Camp Life Is Paradise for Freddy

Ohio University Research in International Studies

This series of publications on Africa, Latin America, Southeast Asia, and Global and Comparative Studies is designed to present significant research, translation, and opinion to area specialists and to a wide community of persons interested in world affairs. The series is distributed worldwide. For more information, consult the Ohio University Press website, ohioswallow.com.

Books in the Ohio University Research in International Studies series are published by Ohio University Press in association with the Center for International Studies. The views expressed in individual volumes are those of the authors and should not be considered to represent the policies or beliefs of the Center for International Studies, Ohio University Press, or Ohio University.

Executive editor: Gillian Berchowitz
Southeast Asia Series consultants: Elizabeth F. Collins and William H. Frederick

Camp Life Is Paradise for Freddy

A Childhood in the Dutch East Indies, 1933–1946

Fred Lanzing
Translated by Marjolijn de Jager
Introduction by William H. Frederick

OHIO UNIVERSITY RESEARCH IN INTERNATIONAL STUDIES
SOUTHEAST ASIA SERIES NO. 131
OHIO UNIVERSITY PRESS
ATHENS

© 2017 by the
Center for International Studies
Ohio University
All rights reserved

To obtain permission to quote, reprint, or otherwise reproduce or distribute material from Ohio University Press publications, please contact our rights and permissions department at (740) 593-1154 or (740) 593-4536 (fax).

Printed in the United States of America

The books in the Ohio University Research in International Studies Series are printed on acid-free paper ♾ ™

27 26 25 24 23 22 21 20 19 18 17   5 4 3 2 1

The title is taken from an entry in the diary of the author's mother, written in May 1944.

The publisher gratefully acknowledges the support of the Dutch Foundation for Literature.

**Nederlands letterenfonds
dutch foundation
for literature**

Library of Congress Cataloging-in-Publication Data
Names: Lanzing, Fred, 1933– author. | De Jager, Marjolijn, translator. | Frederick, William H., writer of introduction.
Title: Camp life is paradise for Freddy : a childhood in the Dutch East Indies, 1933–1946 / Fred Lanzing ; translated by Marjolijn de Jager ; introduction by William H. Frederick.
Other titles: Voor Fredje is het kamp een paradijs. English
Description: Athens, Ohio : Ohio University Press, 2016. | Series: Ohio University research in international studies. Southeast Asia series ; no. 131 | Includes bibliographical references and index.
Identifiers: LCCN 2016048990| ISBN 9780896803077 (hc : alk. paper) | ISBN 9780896803084 (pb : alk. paper) | ISBN 9780896804968 (pdf)
Subjects: LCSH: Lanzing, Fred, 1933——Childhood and youth. | World War, 1939–1945—Concentration camps—Indonesia. | World War, 1939–1945—Prisoners and prisons, Japanese. | World War, 1939–1945—Personal narratives, Dutch. | Dutch—Indonesia—Biography.
Classification: LCC D805.I55 L3613 2016 | DDC 940.53/17598092 [B] —dc23
LC record available at https://lccn.loc.gov/2016048990

Contents

List of Illustrations	vii
Acknowledgments	ix
Note on Spelling	xi
Introduction by William H. Frederick	xiii

ONE	The Dutch East Indies	1
TWO	Surabaya	4
THREE	Buitenzorg	8
FOUR	Batavia	13
FIVE	Batavia, Open City	25
SIX	Kramat	29
SEVEN	Cideng	35
EIGHT	Tangerang	43
NINE	Cimahi	48
TEN	Bandung	61
ELEVEN	Jakarta	64
TWELVE	Adek	67
THIRTEEN	The 10th Battalion	69
FOURTEEN	Tanjung Priok	72
FIFTEEN	Rite of Passage	74
SIXTEEN	Holland	80
	Afterword	87

Appendix: The Questionnaire	93
Glossary	117
About the Author	121
Selected Works by Fred Lanzing	123
Index	125

Illustrations

The author's father receiving a Japanese delegation, June 1941	6
A Surabaya newspaper notice of author's father, August 1939	7
The author with mother and sister, March 1943	33
The house of Captain Sone at the entrance of Cideng Camp	41
Identification photo of Captain Sone after his arrest	56
Captain Sone bows in the Japanese manner for the court-martial	85
Aerial photo of Glodok Prison in Batavia	85

Acknowledgments

Many are those who have stimulated and encouraged me in writing this book. I have much appreciated their interest. There is one who read every version and commented on each. My abundant gratitude for your criticism, suggestions, and loving commitment, Anneloes Timmerije.

Note on Spelling

There have been numerous official spelling changes, to say nothing of shifting language usage, in Indonesia and the Netherlands since the colonial era. The non-English vocabulary used in this book adheres as closely as possible to contemporary spelling standards as represented in the standard dictionaries or lexicons, and attempts to be consistent. This approach does sacrifice a certain amount of nostalgic atmosphere for those acquainted with the prewar period but has the advantage of providing easier entry to the topic for contemporary readers. The Indonesian language does not indicate plurals with a final "s," but for clarity and understanding in English that is how plurals are indicated here: *pemuda* (an activist youth or freedom fighter), *pemuda*s (more than one *pemuda*). Purists will—not without a certain justification—be offended, but again simple clarity for a wide range of readers is the primary goal.

Introduction

In its original 2007 Dutch edition, this book did not require an introduction. Fred Lanzing's compact but powerful memoir of his boyhood in colonial Java, including several years in internment camps during the Japanese occupation, covers territory with which most Dutch readers were at least vaguely acquainted. The memoir begins with a charming and recognizable evocation of *tempo dulu* ("the good old [colonial] days") from a child's perspective but quickly introduces unconventional, even startling, views about what the war and especially the internment camps of the Japanese occupation were actually like. In a concise Afterword the author attempts to explain his outlook and intentions, lest there be any doubt about them. Most Dutch readers, whether or not they agreed with, appreciated, or were willing even to consider Lanzing's challenging conclusions, were at least still on more or less familiar ground.

To readers outside the Netherlands and what might be called the Dutch diaspora, however, the same circumstances do not necessarily obtain, and for this English-language edition some additional background and commentary may be welcome.

Today, three generations after the end of World War II in Southeast Asia (the Pacific War), most of the former Western colonial powers hold respectful but much-faded memories of the civilians who were interned there by Japanese occupation forces. A recent scholarly survey calls them "forgotten captives," and similar language is found in much of the fairly limited academic, journalistic, and autobiographical work that has appeared over the years. Public interest has been, and remains, on military affairs (including military POWs) and the general fate of the colonies, including the connections between Japanese rule and the rise of local independence movements. And in any case, the war in Southeast Asia remains today vastly overshadowed in Western public eyes by events and people in the war as it played out in Europe.

A partial and important exception to this pattern is the Netherlands. There, although the European war and the German occupation that accompanied it clearly receive the bulk of public interest, the Pacific War in the then colonial Netherlands East Indies has, despite periodic complaints to the contrary from some quarters, continued to receive significant attention. A major reason for this difference from the rest of Europe has to do with numbers. In the Netherlands East Indies, about 105,000 Dutch civilians were interned by the Japanese—more than two-thirds were women and children. By comparison, there were roughly 8,000 American internees in the Philippines, 4,000 British in Malaya, and fewer than 200 British and French in Burma and Indochina, respectively. Most of the surviving Dutch civilian internees returned or emigrated to the Netherlands at the end of the war, and they were later joined by an additional 200,000 or more Dutch subjects (a majority of whom were Eurasians), who, though mostly not interned, were badly treated by Japanese policies and wartime conditions, and then targeted in the turbulence that came in the wake of the Pacific War, the Indonesian drive for independence. Together these groups, and eventually their children and grandchildren, make up a significant portion of the Dutch population, more than 3 percent in 2010.

Numbers alone do not tell the entire story, however. From the very beginning of this emigration, disputes arose over issues such as the manner in which the émigrés were received in the Netherlands (many felt it chilly, if not hostile, with little support), the extent to which their experiences were comparable to those of the Dutch in the German-occupied Netherlands, and whether they should be entitled to financial compensation (from whatever source) for property losses, back pay for those who had served in the colonial administration or military, and physical as well as mental suffering. Debate over these and related questions, which was muted at first, became more pronounced at the end of the 1960s, when discussion of what came to be called the "Indies Question" (Indische Kwestie) became more open. At the same time it became entangled with other public debates such as those over the role of the military in the Dutch-Indonesian war ("decolonization") (1945–49) and questions about memorializing World War II (in both Europe and Asia); these in turn were intensified in one way or another by society-wide pressures such as growing ethnic diversity and rising expectations for the government's welfare responsibility. The resulting polemical knot came to be referred to as the nation's *onverwerkte* ("unprocessed" but also "unassimilated" or "unaccepted") colonial past and took on the characteristics of nothing less than a struggle to redefine the Dutch national identity, a struggle that persists today.

At or very near the heart of all this smoldered—and smolders still, seventy years later—the fundamental question of what the wartime experience of the colonial Dutch had actually been like under the Japanese. This is a far more difficult question to answer than might be imagined, especially since "objective" documentation is almost entirely lacking. Whatever historical understanding can be reached must be founded largely on personal sources: diaries (including drawings made at the time), memoirs and interviews written down much later, and literary evocations. Modern historians are well acquainted with the problems of using such sources, which are in this instance compounded by the fact that of roughly 92,000 survivors only at most 1 in 100 (and perhaps considerably fewer) left even short written or recorded accounts. There was from the start a range of views, but the result was an increasingly lopsided public memory war. By the early 1970s the dominant popular understanding, among both the general public in the Netherlands and, apparently, survivors themselves, was that internment under the Japanese had been fully as horrific as the experiences they associated with wartime in the Netherlands, perhaps even worse. It had been, according to this picture, uniformly hellish: three and one half years of extreme deprivation (especially starvation), characterized by extreme violence and all the tools of violence in the hands of diabolical Japanese intent on exterminating Westerners; the experience had been severe enough to scar victims, especially children, irreparably. A few former internees pushed back against this perspective, which they saw as the product of blatant and often dishonest exaggeration, describing it as full of inaccuracies and outright fabrications. The most prominent of these critics was the writer Rudy Kousbroek (1929–2010), who published the first of many pieces (though not a memoir) on the subject as early as 1971 and who coined the term East Indies Camp Syndrome (*Oostindisch Kampsyndroom*) to describe what he believed was a kind of hysterical need to sensationalize—indeed lie about—the Indies wartime experience.

Lanzing's 2007 memoir is the most polished and important of his several contributions to this long-running polemic. Its origins lie in the understated and thoughtful collection of "autobiographical notes," carefully worded and copiously footnoted, that Lanzing published in 1980 in a prominent Dutch journal of letters. Lanzing argued that his own experience as a young boy in wartime Java had not in fact been traumatic and had little in common with the dominant popular view. Far from it. From what he had perceived through a child's eyes, he understood that rather than unrelieved hell, life varied a great deal from camp to camp and from one period to another; even the food situation and hunger levels ranged widely, and in any case were not, until the last months of the occupation, nearly as dire as widely depicted; discomforts, overcrowding, and poor hygienic conditions were undeniable, but many of the problems of camp life were caused or exacerbated by the Dutch camp leaders and internees themselves. As for the Japanese, they were seldom seen and in any case did not appear to have been guilty of the innate cruelty and barbaric behavior commonly reported and believed. Indeed, Lanzing went out of his way to show that in his personal experience even Sone Kenichi, perhaps the most notorious of all Japanese internment officers (executed in 1946 as a war criminal), had displayed shades of empathy and humanity. It had not always been an easy time, Lanzing concluded, but it had paradoxically afforded him great freedoms ("no school, no shoes, no parents"), a certain amount of excitement and adventure, an unusual coming of age that, in retrospect, was an integral part of the colonial childhood that he felt it a privilege to have experienced. The same points are made in the 2007 memoir, but in the framework of a broader, richer, and more chronological narrative, from which the author draws more pointedly critical conclusions.

Both works have attracted hostility. Lanzing has been labeled, among other things, an implicit collaborator ("pro-Jap"), an enemy of national and social solidarity, a person with anticolonial sentiments (as a bad quality), and a disturbed person suffering from "Jap-camp-child syndrome" who is "stuck in pre-puberty characterized by egocentrism." Reviewers have suggested that his work ignores or trivializes the suffering of others, is merely an outdated and vague gesture rather than anything substantive, flies in the face of the demonstrated real-life experiences of thousands of children and adults who were interned, or—perhaps as devastating in its own way as any other criticism—amounts to nothing more than a "silly book." (A few, to be fair, found the memoir vaguely "compelling," or "interesting," for details not found anywhere else in the literature.) The more extreme reactions are obviously highly emotionally charged, and the rest often appear to ignore or misunderstand precisely what Lanzing is or is not saying. But their nature is serious enough, and Lanzing's mission to correct the record important enough, that they deserve at least brief comment here.

A prime set of concerns has to do with historical accuracy. Memoirs are not history, of course, nor memory truth, and certainly the idea (from which Lanzing draws much inspiration) that the child's view of things, being presumably free of adult preconceptions and expectations, reflects a more authentic memory, may be more literary than historical and is in any case open to serious question. Nevertheless, it must be said that from a historian's perspective the picture of Dutch internment presented in Lanzing's memoir is in fact considerably closer to that of careful scholarly assessment than is the dominant popular version, especially that found in literature and the cinema. He is certainly correct to highlight the variability of conditions according to time, place, and individual circumstances, for example, particularly where the infamous Cideng camp—invariably considered representative, which it emphatically was not—is concerned. (In Java alone there were initially over one hundred different camps, later consolidated to about thirty.) And his account of the Japanese presence, actions, and intentions in the camps is not out of line with most even-handed research on the subject going back as far as Van Velden's classic 1963 work on the internments. Few serious scholars of the Japanese occupation today would have any basic quarrels with Lanzing's 1985 generalization, of which the memoir is intended to provide an illustration, that

> the clichéd image of cruel "Japs," with constant rapes, deliberate liquidations of Europeans, and three straight years of hunger, death, and destruction, with people eating sand and grass, and guards playing macabre games with the [European] women, and so forth—as if this was the daily reality of the internment camp—is, I maintain, false. [Life in] the average [civilian] internment camp was characterized by boredom, quarrels and disputes [among internees], uncertainty, incomprehensible regulations, lack of privacy and hygiene, hopelessness, and also, toward the end, a shortage of food.

Lanzing is also reliable where important specific details are concerned. To take only one example, he is right to emphasize that Cideng camp was not an armed fortress and did not have watchtowers manned by machine-gun-armed guards, contrary to the claims in Jeroen Brouwers's *Bezonken rood* (*Sunken Red*) (1981) and many other works, including those by a number of former internees there. A few similar points may be slightly in doubt, such as whether the Cideng camp fencing incorporated barbed wire. Lanzing, who took part in the original construction, says it did not; another internee, a young adult tasked with repairing the fencing (perhaps after Lanzing had left), has reported that it did; photographs taken at war's end are for several reasons slightly in doubt. These kinds of contradictions are common in camp histories and often cannot be resolved with complete certainty. But the basic point is sound: even the worst of the Japanese internment sites for civilians was far from the Nazi-style prison bastion it has been widely depicted as resembling. Seemingly a comparatively small matter, though one of some importance if rigorous truth-telling about the internment experience is at issue. (As an aside, it should also be pointed out that Lanzing certainly wasn't the only person at the time or later to think that many of the Dutch trials at the war's end condemning Japanese to death as war criminals were vengeful and less than just, and even Allied representative Laurens van der Post, in a 1985 letter, said he believed Sone was a man with "an individual sense of honour and decency" whom he had "tried very hard to prevent . . . from being executed as a common criminal.")

It is perfectly reasonable to ask whether, if Lanzing's account is fundamentally credible and accurate, the same or similar information and views have been expressed in other survivors' autobiographical works, and if not, why not. The answer to the first part of the question is that they have, but infrequently. The corpus of personal documents shows enormous variety and remains incompletely studied, so generalizations about them must be tentative. But there were diary writers who clearly made an effort to question gossip and avoid extreme opinions or descriptions, perhaps out of fear of retribution if their writings (which were forbidden) were discovered, but also because, it would seem, they believed that keeping a balanced and realistic view was a key to survival. (By contrast, memoirs composed after the war, sometimes many decades later, by those who had been interned as adults seem more often to show heightened emotions, inaccurate information, and intensely anti-Japanese sentiments.) Memoirs by ex-internees who spent childhood years in the camps are in large part compromised, sometimes seriously so, by the authors' efforts to supplement their own limited memories (many were very young) with information and attitudes taken from interviews and the reading of other accounts; only a comparatively small number, no more than a dozen or so, make a serious effort to sort out what they knew, thought, and felt at the time from what they learned later from others. Fred Lanzing's memoir is one of the latter group. These authors show us a less dramatic camp life than popularly portrayed, and one in which children's lives differ considerably from prewar times: they are freer of adult supervision, have more time on their hands to "play" or do adventurous things, but often take on adult responsibilities and attitudes. They are conscious of the maturity that circumstances force upon them and frequently are critical of their parents and other adults. They acknowledge the scarcity of food but do not see that as a central issue. Most noticeably, the Japanese are not a focus of their concern, much less hatred. In these accounts they are seldom seen and figure less frequently as the barbarous villains many of their parents often saw, and more as part of a vaguely uncertain and often puzzling human landscape. The children do not spend much time looking back to prewar days and longing for a return to them, or expecting a particular future.

The memoirs that come closest to mirroring Lanzing's view are those by Ernest Hillen (*The Way of a Boy: A Memoir of Java*, 1993) and Jan Lechner (*Uit de Verte: Een jeugd in Indië 1927–1946* [From a distance: A youth in the Indies, 1927–1946], 2004). Both are longer and in some ways more detailed accounts, but the young lives and perspectives they depict are powerful confirmation of much of what Lanzing tells us. Hillen, for example, recalls that "for me the worst thing about living in [the internment] camp was not the heat, fear, smells, noise, flies, too many bodies, too little food, scratches that festered, and diarrhea—it was the sameness." He disagrees with adults and the values they sometimes try to enforce, and wants them to recognize that he, at nine or ten, is no longer a child: "I wasn't a kid. I didn't pee, I pissed. You didn't give things away—[certainly] not food; you traded." Hillen doesn't say directly that internment was a privilege to have experienced, but he is very far from suggesting that it was a trauma. Lechner, who was a few years older than Lanzing and Hillen, nevertheless shows us a camp life that is very similar, and certainly not a misery. He hears and witnesses Japanese violence against Europeans, but insists that was not usual in the camps. And he notes that he has wondered in retrospect why he never developed "a total, enduring, and blinding hatred of the Japanese," but he did not. Like Lanzing, Lechner also sees his wartime experience as on the whole a positive experience, preparing him well for embarking on his adult life.

As to the second part of the question, it is not clear why there are not more accounts from former camp children that corroborate the picture we get from Lanzing and the others. It doesn't seem possible that only a minuscule number of the more than 27,000 child survivors saw things in more or less the same way, or that they represent only very rare exceptions due to blind luck, special treatment, or extraordinary psychological circumstances (healthy or otherwise). More likely, their perspective is more widely shared, but others have declined to write about it, either because they believed it was unnecessary or unimportant to do so, or because they did not wish to bring attention to themselves, especially by contradicting what had become the received popular view. A Dutch researcher recently discovered how real such pressures may have been when she was informed by several former camp children, now well in their eighties, that their parents had forbidden them to say such outlandish things as that they had felt free and had rather pleasant memories of life in the internment camps; they never realized that others might have had the same feelings, and they certainly never dared express them in public, until they heard of Lanzing's memoir many decades later. A few individuals have indicated their approval directly to Lanzing, but not spoken or written publicly about it. Some accounts from former camp children in places like Hong Kong and Manila reflect similar experiences and thoughts.

Introduction xxi

There is a decided irony here, perhaps easily missed by readers unfamiliar with the terms of the continuing debate in the Netherlands over the occupation. The understanding long established in popular myth about the Japanese occupation of the Indies holds that the full force of the "truth" of that experience—the awful truth of unvarying savagery, misery, and so forth—was and still is silenced, and its victims must struggle to be heard. Not only is that at best an exaggeration, but it seems fair to say that something like the opposite has in fact been the case: in the popular arena it is the "benign" views that have been hushed, given short shrift, or dismissed altogether as merely contrarian. The sensationalist popular view, in contrast, now extends to second and third generations whose often spectacularly inaccurate grasp of history proliferates even in more or less official publications, and whose politics appear to make closure regarding the colonial past—and, it must be said, full accommodation of a multicultural present—very difficult indeed.

Fred Lanzing's memoir is a remarkable and thought-provoking work, notable for its determination to present a factually and emotionally accurate account of the author's childhood internment, and with it to provide a credible modification of or counterweight to popular mythology and what he sees as a "failed, one-sided, and sterile processing of the war experiences in the Dutch East Indies." That effort has unquestionably required among other things courage and a thick skin, as well as a certain stubbornness in the face of the realization that it is not likely to succeed in its main purpose. For the historian or historically inclined reader, however, the memoir remains not only a literary pleasure but a key source for understanding the Japanese occupation in Indonesia. It is also of special interest as one of the rare personal sources daring to speak so bluntly about both the realities of war in the Indies and the implications of the subsequent seventy-year-old memory wars that followed. This is a work that deserves an attentive audience outside its native Netherlands.

William H. Frederick

Selected Sources and Further Reading

Blackburn, Kevin, and Karl Hack, eds. *Forgotten Captives in Japanese-Occupied Asia*. London: Routledge, 2008.

Brouwers, Jeroen. *Bezonken rood*. Amsterdam: Arbeiders Pers, 1981. Translated as *Sunken Red*. New York: New Amsterdam, 1988.

Captain, Esther. *Achter het kawat was Nederland: Indisch oorlogservaringen en -herinneringen 1942–1995* [The Netherlands behind barbed wire: Indisch war experiences and recollections, 1942–1995]. Kampen: Kok, 2002.

———. "'Geen spoortje Indisch, geen bamboe, geen prikkeldraad'" ['No sign of Indisch, no bamboo, no barbed wire']. In Kristel, *Binnenskamers*, 325–55.

Dütting, Hans, ed. *Over Jeroen Brouwers: Kritische motieven: Beschouwingen over het werk van Jeroen Brouwers* [On Jeroen Brouwers: Critical motifs: Considerations of the work of Jeroen Brouwers]. Baarn: De Prom, 1987.

Ernest Hillen. *The Way of a Boy: A Memoir of Java*. 1993. New York: Penguin 1995.

Hoek, Jasper van der. "'Geen haat, maar afkeer': Japanse kampbewakers in de ogen van geïnterneerden in Nederlands-Indië; een vergelijking van dagboeken, memoires en interviews" ['Not hate, but aversion': Japanese camp guards in the eyes of internees in the Dutch East Indies; a comparison of diaries, memoirs and interviews]. Master's thesis in social history. Rotterdam: Erasmus University, 2006.

Kemperman, Jeroen. *De Japanse bezetting in dagboeken: Tjideng* [The Japanese occupation in diaries: Cideng]. Amsterdam, NIOD, 2002.

Kousbroek, Rudy. *Het Oostindisch kampsyndroom* [The East Indies camp syndrome]. Amsterdam: Meulenhof, 1992.

Kristel, Connie, ed. *Binnenskamers: Terugkeer en opvang na de Tweede Wereldoorlog* [In private: Return and relief after the Second World War]. Amsterdam: Bert Bakker, 2002.

Lechner, Jan. *Uit de Verte: Een jeugd in Indië, 1927–1946* [From a distance: A youth in the Indies, 1927–1946]. Leiden: KITLV, 2004.

Leffelaar, Hendrik L. *Through a Harsh Dawn: A Boy Grows Up in a Japanese Prison Camp*. Barre, MA: Barre Publishing, 1963.

Locher-Scholten, Elsbeth. "After the 'Distant War': Dutch Public Memory of the Second World War in Asia." In Raben, *Representing*, 105–28.

Mul, Sarah de. "Nostalgia for Empire: 'Tempo Doeloe' in Contemporary Dutch Literature." *Memory Studies* 3, no. 4 (2010): 413–28.

Ockerse, Ralph, and Evelijn Blaney. *Our Childhood in the Former Colonial Dutch East Indies: Recollections before and during Our Wartime Internment by the Japanese.* Bloomington, IN: Xlibris, 2011.

Oort, Boudewijn van. *Tjideng Reunion: A Memoir of World War II in Java.* Victoria, BC: Trafford, 2008.

Oostindie, Geert. *Postcolonial Netherlands: Sixty-Five Years of Forgetting, Commemorating, Silencing.* Amsterdam: University of Amsterdam Press, 2011.

Post, Peter, et al., eds. *The Encyclopedia of Indonesia in the Pacific War.* Leiden: Brill, 2010.

Raben, Remco. "Dutch Memories of Captivity in the Pacific War." In Blackburn and Hack, *Forgotten Captives*, 94–110.

Raben, Remco, ed. *Representing the Japanese Occupation of Indonesia.* Zwolle: Waanders/NIOD, 1999.

Rinzema, Win. *Dit was uw Tjideng: Aspecten van de vertraagde afwikkeling van Japanse interneringskampen in Batavia met het Tjidengkamp als casus* [This was you, Cideng: Aspects of the delayed dissolution of Japanese internment camps in Batavia, with Cideng as a case study]. 1989. Utrecht: Stichting Icodo, 1991.

Tijn, Joop van. "Een jongen, van éen tot dertien" [A boy, from one to thirteen]. In *Het einde van Indië: Indische Nederlanders tijdens de Japanse bezetting en de dekolonisatie* [The end of the Indies: The Indies Dutch during the Japanese occupation and decolonization], edited by Wim Willems and Jaap de Moor, 51–59. The Hague: Sdu Uitgeverij Koninginnegracht, 1995.

Velden, D. van. *De Japanse burgerkampen* [The Japanese civilian internment camps]. 1963. 4th printing. Franeker: Wever, 1985.

Chapter 1

THE DUTCH EAST INDIES

It is a fact that it takes experience before one can realize what is a catastrophe and what is not. Children have little faculty of distinguishing between disaster and the ordinary course of their lives.
—Robert Hughes, *A High Wind in Jamaica*

Children see and hear what is there; adults see and hear what they are expected to and mainly remember what they think they ought to remember.
—David Lowenthal, *The Past Is a Foreign Country*

I was born and grew up before, during, and right after the Pacific War in the Dutch East Indies, a colony of the Netherlands, and I can't imagine being born under luckier stars. I was a *totok*, a child born in the Indies of European parents. Colonial society was my everyday environment.

My life took place at school, in the yard, on the street, and around the so-called outbuildings where the *gudangs*, the storage rooms, were, and where the servants lived with their families. I would play between the stalls and baskets in the marketplace, the *pasar*, and during school vacations I'd roam around the green mountainsides of the Preanger region with its tea plantations. My daily surroundings were full of sounds: human voices, the dull snorting of water buffalo, the tinkling of the little bells on the small carriage horses, birds singing, insects buzzing, and the quacking of a raft of ducks, while somewhere around there was always a rooster crowing. When I watch a TV broadcast about Indonesia, I'm always expecting a cock's call in the distance. And it's always there; you can bet your life on it.

There were smells. The smell of people and animals, the mucky odor of the brown river water, the scent of piles of papayas and mangoes in the market, the rotting smell of *trasi,* a shrimp paste that every native inhabitant of the country is wild about, the sweetish sugarcane aroma of *gula jawa,* which is prepared in bamboo tubes and always contains small twigs and cockroaches that fall in during the cooking. And above all, the omnipresent odor everywhere, the mixture of manure, decaying fruit, and smoldering smoke, an aroma that even today hangs suspended in the small cities and the *desas,* the villages, and that fills you with bittersweet joy each time you smell it, no matter what your age.

I had contact with the people of the land every day: Sundanese and Javanese and, as they were officially referred to, "Foreign Asians": Hindus from British India, Chinese, Iraqis (who were actually Mesopotamian Jews), and Arabs from Yemen and Hadramaut. They dressed and behaved differently, and they lived in a world of which I really had no clue. They spoke languages I didn't understand, but everyone made do with market Malay, myself included.

As a child I had no concept of what a colonial society stood for. I felt at home in this country and among its population with the authenticity of someone born there. I knew no better. Much later on, looking back at that time, I would think on occasion: What were we actually doing there? By what right were the Dutch there? Weren't we merely foreigners who were neglecting the population and basically exploiting the land for our own profit? In 1940 in all of the Dutch East Indies, as I now know, there were 221 Indonesian physicians and 230 academics out of a population of sixty million. That is nothing to be proud of. But on a personal level I don't feel guilty about it. It is history; it is just the way things were.

I'm not inclined to apologize to the Indonesians for what happened during the colonial era. Besides, they aren't asking for any apologies. By the same token, I don't feel the need to have the Japanese apologize to me for what happened in the Pacific War. Some of my ex-companions in adversity have been whining about that for decades and will probably continue to do so.

As a child I never really saw any Indonesian businesspeople, teachers, doctors, or intellectuals. They didn't come to our house. I didn't know they existed.

From November 1939 onward, my father was the aide-de-camp of Governor-General Tjarda van Starkenborgh Stachouwer.[1] Because of my father's position he and my mother were obliged to attend many audiences and official functions. At one of these my mother met the wife of an indigenous regent. She came from the upper Javanese *priyayi* aristocracy and, as my mother ironically commented, spoke a more polished Dutch than many Europeans in the colony. The two women became friends, insofar as circumstances allowed. They never visited each other, presumably because the Indonesian woman didn't consider it proper: my parents weren't chic enough.

In this book I recount my youth in the Dutch East Indies from 1933 to 1946. I have many childhood memories, memories of my life as a boy in Japanese internment camps and of the first few months after the liberation.

The events are almost photographically imprinted in my mind. And I still know very clearly what my thoughts were when I saw something happen, or when I heard or experienced something.

My story is not being told by a victim.

My colonial youth and the Pacific War have shaped me profoundly. For me this confusing and unforgettable time is a privilege that fate—or chance—simply dropped into my lap.

---

1. The governor-general was the representative of the Queen of the Netherlands in the Dutch East Indies.

Chapter 2

SURABAYA

Rain would fall in the afternoon. First it would grow dark with heavy, low-hanging clouds. Everything grew silent, and then you'd hear the rustling of the rain's arrival. When the first drops hit the dusty ground, a heavy smell of soil arose from the earth, lasting only a few seconds. Shortly thereafter, the water would pelt and rattle on the shingles of the roofs and on the gravel, and gurgle through the drains and gutters. Just above the ground a slight mist of splashing drops would form. Every once in a while we were allowed to play in the rain. Naked and whooping, we'd then jump around in the abundant water falling straight down from the sky. The servants' children stood in the doorway of their quarters and watched us in amazement. Who would be crazy enough to run around in the rain! It undoubtedly reinforced their own and their parents' conviction that the *belandas*—the Dutch—had a screw loose.

In the evenings in the rainy season a thick cloud of *larons,* flying ants, would sometimes come plummeting down abruptly around the lamps. The humidity was causing the larvae to come out by the thousands from their eggs in the ground. They were gross and fat and whitish with transparent wings. It was the light of the floor lamp on the terrace that attracted them. They'd hit against the hot lamp and then fall thrashing to the ground. The servants caught them in a *wajan,* a large round iron pan we know as a wok, and fry them in their own fat. They considered it a delicacy.

Later the frogs would come to life again, croaking loudly into the night. Sometimes they'd suddenly fall silent all at the same time as if they were being directed by a mysterious conductor. Tucked away safely beneath your mosquito net, you'd listen to them.

At that moment the street vendors with their foodstuffs came by the homes. They had many customers in the European neighborhoods, too, because their merchandise was cheap and very tasty. You'd hear the recurrent, grinding squeak of the carrying pole they used to transport their wares. With a pounding heart you'd wait for their long-drawn-out melancholy call with which they recommended their dishes. The sound could fill you with a nameless shiver. And then the small oil lamp's flickering flame would throw a ghostly pattern of light and shadow across the window as you lay trembling in your bed.

We were living in Surabaya; it was 1939, and I was six years old. My father was supply corps officer of the KNIL.[2] He was responsible for the purchase of everything the army needed, from rice to clothing, from hardware to textiles, from footwear to soap.

He received the suppliers at his office in the *tangsi,* the barracks. They were always Chinese wholesalers, often accompanied by a nattily dressed young assistant, whose job it was to take notes in a little book or work out estimates on an abacus worn glossy from wear and tear.

At New Year's and other celebrations these suppliers had gifts delivered to our home, such as fireworks, trinkets, delicacies, or a little basket with birds' nests. My father would only accept small gifts, for in this society bribery was a frequently employed practice. When he was promoted to the rank of major, a magnificently adorned and lusciously prepared suckling pig was delivered to our house that very same evening. It was presented on an enormous, precious silver platter decorated with many artfully engraved ringlets and rosettes. The little animal had been arranged wholly intact on a bed of vegetables and fruit. What especially fascinated me was the pineapple he was holding in his snout. We ate the piglet with relish to the barely concealed disgust of the servants who, like most Javanese, were Muslim.

---

2. KNIL: Royal Netherlands East Indies Army.

The next day my father sent the *jongos,* the houseboy, to the downtown office of the Chinese to return the gigantic platter. Still clutching it in his arms, he came back an hour later with the message: "The *Cina* says there's a misunderstanding, *Tuan,*" he said with lowered eyes, trying to shove the platter into my father's hands. But my father knew all too well what he could open himself up for with gifts such as these. "Once I get involved this way there'll be no end to it," he said; "it should stop with something insignificant." That same platter went back and forth a few more times before the Chinese man gave up.

My father was a devoted equestrian. Next to the outbuildings behind the house was a stable with two horses. They were cared for by a *spandri;* this was a soldier close to retirement age who would be put into service for small chores. I liked going into the stable. It smelled nice, and the old man would be quietly busying himself with the

My father at work, formally receiving the second Japanese economic delegation and guiding them up the stairs of the palace of Governor-General Tjarda van Starkenborgh Stachouwer in former Batavia in June 1941. The man at the center is the diplomat Yoshizawa. During the banquet that evening, Yoshizawa invited my mother for a spree in Batavia nightlife. To encourage her, he presented her with a beautiful silver cigarette box. My mother declined politely. The silver box is still in my possession.

My father in the *Soerabaiasch Handelsblad* of August 30, 1939, on the occasion of his appointment as aide-de-camp to the governor-general.

animals, to which he talked uninterruptedly while the bats would swoosh high up in the beams. I'd sit on a little bench and watch him, the odor of the horses' fresh sweat, urine, and leather all around me.

My father rode every morning, no matter how late it might have been the night before. In the early dawn the stableboy was waiting for him next to the house, holding the reins of a horse restlessly shaking his head, scraping the pavement stones with his hooves.

After the ride the horse was wet with sweat, and his bit would be foaming. Sometimes his flank showed lashes from which drops of blood were welling up. He had been insubordinate during the jumps, and it was no use going up against my father, a rigid man, with that kind of behavior.

On 30 August 1939, the house was filled with flowers, and on the terrace the champagne corks were popping. My father had been named to the position of aide-de-camp to Governor-General Tjarda van Starkenborgh Stachouwer. A few weeks later we moved to Buitenzorg.

Surabaya 7

Chapter 3

BUITENZORG

Buitenzorg[3] was still a very small town in 1939. This is where the governor-general traditionally resided, although most of the government services were located in Batavia. The small white palace was set in a spacious park on a hill. Guards stood at the entrance gate. About twenty deer were grazing on the large lawn. There were big ponds behind the palace, and then the land ran imperceptibly into the colonial botanical gardens.

I accompanied my mother a few times on her visits to this palace. Although it was by no means large, it was spaciously constructed with high ceilings and had an appealing aristocratic simplicity. The atmosphere was relaxed. The guards, the gardeners, and the servants were all extremely friendly. I liked going there. Years later, I learned that it had been President Sukarno's favorite residence, a choice I can appreciate. Later still, I heard that President Suharto hadn't dared set foot in there because it was the site of choice for Sukarno's ghost to wander around at night. This, too, is a choice I can appreciate. Besides, I suspect that the ghost spent more time roaming around inside Suharto's conscience than in the hallways of that charming little palace.

We lived in Buitenzorg for only a few months. We moved into a house on a hill just outside the residential area. It was a lovely house surrounded by a large garden. The living room had a little bar and even a fireplace. It had been the mayor's house, my parents said.

In 1940 the Sitzkrieg in Europe had turned into a true Blitzkrieg. The Netherlands was occupied by the Germans. Japan waged a

---

3. Buitenzorg is currently known as Bogor.

merciless war in China, and for its designs of conquest in the entire Pacific region it had a great need of raw materials and oil, which it didn't have at home. However, the Dutch East Indies did, and one way or the other Japan wanted to gain control of these.

The governor-general would frequently go to Batavia, always accompanied by his staff. My father was therefore often away from home.

Every now and then my parents rented a bungalow in the Preanger, in the mountains of West Java. We would go there during school vacations and sometimes for weekends to "catch a breath of fresh air." The little wooden house was close to a vast tea plantation that belonged to one of my uncles. He lived there with his family, whose two sons were just about my age. Covering the hillsides all around were pale green tea gardens.

I was always up early. Then I'd go to my uncle's large house near the factory. At the break of day the morning wind would rustle through the stands of dry bamboo. In the pale sky a few stars were still visible. You could smell the dew on the soil that lay steaming in the first rays of the sun while gently waving spirals of charcoal smoke floated through the air. The coolies were sitting beside the shed by the light of smoldering oil lamps, and, crouching on their heels, the women pickers were waiting for the day's instructions. In hushed almost comradely tones my uncle consulted with the *mandurs,* the supervisors and foremen, who then nodded that they understood, but they'd also make suggestions, to which my uncle listened attentively.

After everyone had gone to work, my uncle showed his sons and me fresh mud tracks on the tiles of the covered landing behind the house. They were panther tracks. The big cat had been snooping around during the night. I thought it was exciting and looked forward to the envy my schoolmates would show when hearing the story.

During the day it was hot. My cousins and I used to play all day long in a small, cold mountain river filled with boulders, rapids, and eddies. In deeper spots the water was stagnant, and there tiny skittish fish swam around that simply wouldn't let themselves be caught. On the banks we'd catch green frogs and light blue dragonflies that jumped and flew around in vast numbers. We built little dams with stones and twigs. I can't begin to imagine a nicer place to play for seven- and eight-year-old boys.

Sometimes we followed the little brook upriver right to the spring, which was a damp, mossy place, surrounded by ferns amid trees with a dim filtered light passing through. Clear water came burbling from the ground; the atmosphere was mysterious and magical. According to the local people, some benevolent water spirits were living there, which seemed—and still seems—highly plausible to me.

Other days we wandered through the tea plantations where in the mornings the pickers were working. In the hot sun they'd talk listlessly beneath their large woven bamboo hats with cloths attached to protect their neck and upper arms from the sun's rays. They rarely paid any attention to us, unless they were chanting singsong lyrics in chorus when they would cast a sideways ironic glance in our direction. According to my uncle, these were rather lewd Sundanese folk songs. Despite our insistence he refused to translate them. I still hold that against him; how I'd love to be able to sing them today.

One day I was allowed to come along to a *selamatan,* a banquet. This selamatan was held to celebrate the opening of a new tea-drying shed. True to tradition, it was open only to men. When evening fell, my father and I went there. Gritting her teeth and green with envy, my sister, Carolien, watched us leave. But the *adat,* the custom, was inexorable. When I sneeringly looked back at her one more time, she stuck her tongue out at me.

The banquet took place in the open air. The mood was calm. Everyone sat on the ground. Some dishes were served on a banana leaf, others in small bowls. The men were talking in muffled voices.

High above us was the firmament with millions of stars. Torches crackled and smoldered. The lights of fireflies were glowing in the tree branches, and every now and then a big beetle would soar through the air with a rattling swirl. As one of the guests of honor, my father sat at some distance away, having first entrusted me to one of the foremen. I sat in the grass next to this mandur with my legs crossed under me, which at the time was not a problem for me. Unfortunately, I later lost this useful skill.

It was all very exciting, and I was looking around inquisitively to see and experience as much as I possibly could. I really felt *senang,* very content. But to my great shock I suddenly saw a huge pool of blood no more than two meters away from me, at its center the enormous head of a water buffalo that had been sacrificed shortly before. The silky eyes were wide open, and the head rested diagonally on one of the strong horns. I shuddered and involuntarily leaned against the mandur's muscular thigh. Through the fabric of his sarong I felt the reassuring warmth of his skin. If I believed in God, I would want Him to have a warm thigh like that.

A few weeks later we went up into the cool mountains again for several days. Early in the evening we usually sat on the bungalow's large wooden balcony. My parents would read papers and magazines or listen to the radio. Carolien and I played Sorry or made drawings with colored pencils by Caran d'Ache. I often sharpened them with a pencil sharpener because of the delicious wood scent it created.

High up in the sky, lighted from below by the setting sun, clusters of *kalongs,* large bats also known as flying dogs, were moving off to their feeding places. It was cool, and the screeching of the monkeys in the trees farther on only accentuated the silence. Although there were almost no mosquitoes at this elevation—we slept without netting and during the night would pull up a light blanket—on the floor a dot of the *obat nyamuk* glowed softly, a small spiral of some green substance that, smoldering slowly, spreads an incense-like smell, chasing away the mosquitoes.

Suddenly I heard my father say "goddamn" in a half-whisper, while he gazed intently at my uncle who'd just stopped by. The newscaster of the NIROM, the Netherlands Indies Radio Broadcasting Network, had just read the announcement of the sinking caused by Japanese torpedoes in the South China Sea of the British battleships *Prince of Wales* and *Repulse*, which were supposed to be protecting Singapore. It was 10 December 1941. The Dutch East Indies was wide open to invasion by the Japanese fleet.

The footsteps of Mars rang loud and clear.

Chapter 4

BATAVIA

In 1941 political and military tensions in the Pacific were mounting. In order to cope with every contingency, early in the year the entire governmental apparatus of the Indies was centralized in Batavia.[4] We, too, had moved there. We lived on the Sunda Road, a street in Kebon Sirih, the European district just south of the Koningsplein. Batavia was a large city. We were living in a freestanding one-story house surrounded by a garden, modern for its time, as were all the homes in that neighborhood. The house wasn't big, but spacious enough for a family with two children. Facing the street was the terrace where we had tea late in the afternoon and where in the evening company was received. Across from us on the other side of the street was the athletic field of a school. This wasn't the school I attended; I went to the Jan Ligthart School, a few streets further down. The back of the house had an airy covered walkway that led to the kitchen, the bathroom, and the gudangs. And all the way in the back of the yard, beyond the garage, stood the outbuildings. Of course, we had four or five local servants, as did everyone else. They occupied a series of small rooms in the outbuildings. Some had relatives or immediate family members with them. My parents didn't know who exactly was living there, but I don't think it concerned them very much.

The servants moved through the house and across the grounds without a sound. They were always solicitous and patient with us. The maid wore her black hair in a large knot. Her clothes were freshly laundered and smelled of starch in the morning. I don't

---

4. Batavia is now known as Jakarta.

remember her ever punishing me or my sister or ever being irritable. We spoke Dutch with her. When we'd ask: "How old are you?" she would say: "I'm not old and I'm not young; I have always been here."

My parents were accustomed to hiring servants who understood Dutch and were able to speak it to some degree as well. I don't know what their motivation for this was, but I sorely regret it because it prevented us from learning any of the country's languages. Even our marketplace Malay was clumsy. To this day I'm still jealous of cousins of mine who grew up on a plantation and thus learned to speak Sundanese or Javanese from their indigenous playmates.

The correct wage for servants was a perpetual topic of conversation among the European adults. It fluctuated between ten and twenty guilders a month, plus room and board. To say anything meaningful about its level today is rather pointless except for the following, perhaps. On Sunday *koki,* the cook, would customarily make *rijsttafel* for us. My mother would send her to the pasar in the morning to get the necessary ingredients. The koki would buy a chicken, eggs, different vegetables, fish, peppers, oil, a few pounds of rice, and coconuts. For these purchases my mother would give her the amount of one Dutch guilder, which was enough for everything on the shopping list. If koki had a few cents left, she was allowed to keep those. You can rest assured that she'd bargain the vendors down to almost nothing.

In the kitchen the cooking was done on charcoal, *arang,* in braziers, *anglos,* solid cast-iron chafing dishes. Early in the afternoon koki sorted, washed, and cut up the vegetables and chopped the meat. She spoke quietly with her assistant, a little mouse of a girl who was always in her vicinity. And then you'd hear the sound of the rhythmic *kipas,* the bamboo fan, and a smell of charcoal would waft around and prickle your nose, while from time to time small crackling sparks whizzed by.

The water well was in the backyard, near the servants' quarters. Toward the end of the afternoon both men and women would bathe there. One time I was sitting with one of the boys next door on the wall that encircled the water supply. We were watching the people bathing. They crouched down so we wouldn't be able to see their nudity and waited silently and patiently until we left. I'm still ashamed of this because they were too polite (or afraid) to chase us away.

It happened only once. Sastro, the driver, an even-tempered man of about forty who was highly esteemed by my parents, most respectfully asked my father for an appointment, where he spoke about my behavior at the water well. My father, who himself had been raised in the Indies, always approached the native kids, as he referred to them, with respect, something that was not self-evident for most Europeans. And he completely understood. In Sastro's presence I was given a harsh and well-deserved dressing down.

Like all adults, my parents used to retire in the early afternoon heat for a siesta. That was when the garden became our territory. Actually, the children were also supposed to rest, but freedom called, and the heat didn't bother us. Nobody paid any attention to us, which was most agreeable. We'd make sure not to make any noise and played in the yard in our loose flannel pajamas.

Stretched out to their full length, the cats—I don't know how many of them used to roam in and around our house—lay dozing on the cool tiles in the shade or sleeping beneath the bushes. Keenly focused on anything that moved, their playful kittens were chasing butterflies or tapping at beetles and spinning them around.

The nameless crippled duck that had just appeared in our yard one day all tattered, his scrawny body full of messy quills, and without any respect for anything or anyone had chosen our place as his residence, was quacking for attention.

The clatter of the bucket at the well signaled that siesta time was over. The *kebun,* the gardener, would fill two large square oilcans with water and, the muscles of his bare back bulging, carry them into the yard on a pole across his shoulders. When he reached the flowerbeds, he'd pour the water into a smaller can with a wooden handle, whose bottom had been pierced with little holes. Then he'd water the plants, dousing the shrubs and trees as well.

It was time for our bath. In the cool semidark bathroom with its always slightly musty smell, you scooped the water from a huge cement basin, the *mandi*-basin, and poured it over your head. Sometimes the water contained droves of mosquito larvae. To repel them our neighbors kept a few goldfish in their mandi-basin. I loved the looks of that and whined that I wanted the same. But my parents didn't think it was sanitary, and that was the end of the matter.

As you were bathing, you stood on a wooden pallet, which felt mossy and slippery to your bare feet. It was a disagreeable sensation, all the more so because almost transparent, glassy-looking centipedes often lived underneath the pallet. After the bath the maid would use sweetish-smelling baby powder for your neck, between your legs, and between your toes. Then you were allowed to play outside again.

When the kebun had finished watering the plants, he'd languidly rake the gravel path or sweep the hallway and gallery with a *sapu lidi,* a broom made of bendable palm-leaf ribs.

Sometimes he'd carve a slingshot for us from a fork-shaped branch. A frightful weapon. With small round pebbles we'd shoot at sparrows or alley cats that dared venture into our yard. I must confess that I was actually quite happy we never hit anything because I wouldn't have known what to do with an animal injured like that.

When it was kite-flying time, he helped us put together the kites we had bought from the Chinese. He did this with solemn devotion. He also helped us make glass filament from rope, starch, and finely ground glass. Every boy flew his kite with glass filament so he'd be able to cut through the string of other kite flyers during aerial competitions. The gardener gave us pointers on how to launch the kite and on maneuvers needed to protect our fragile structures from the small fighter kites that rose defiantly from a nearby city kampung. Despite his muscular body he was a gentle soul. I suspect he was only a few years older than I, sixteen or seventeen perhaps, and that he took the same childlike joy in flying kites that I did. He addressed me as *sinyo,* and I called him—as did everyone—by his nickname N'tok. I never asked myself whether that was his actual name, whether he was related to one of the other servants, or where he came from. He was simply there.

In the small and narrow tiled gallery in front of their quarters the women prepared their own meal when the day was done. There was a round suspended birdcage with a black mynah bird that would peck at a piece of papaya with such fury that the red splatters flew around everywhere.

Late in the afternoon Sastro, the *sopir,* driver, the jongos, the kebun, and a few family members who didn't work for us used to sit in the shade of the door opening of the garage where it was cool. Sastro could read and used to read out loud from a local newspaper to the other men who listened with rapt attention. Sometimes they'd talk very excitedly all at the same time. In all likelihood they were reacting to reports on the war. Japan had become a great power in the Pacific and wasn't letting itself be bullied by the British or the Americans. It promoted "Asia for the Asians." I think that very few Europeans grasped what this unleashed in the souls of the indigenous population. In any case, I had no inkling of it at the time. I'd wait patiently until they were finished reading the paper because then I'd get to play an important role in this group. I had a comic book of *Flash Gordon* with me as well as the Edgar Rice Burroughs book *Tarzan of the Apes.* I would read the text in Dutch, Sastro would translate, and the men would listen. Chickens scurried about, a friendly cat was pushed away. I could smell the pungent odor of the thin, tapering clove cigarettes.

Nevertheless, in this idyllic colonial picture it didn't escape my notice that sometimes, when they left the premises on an evening off, they'd wear the *kopiah,* a kind of fez, which was the round black head-covering that Sukarno always wore, as a symbol of nationalism. Although it did attract my attention, I don't know if my parents were aware of it, but I never said anything about it.

One day I was sitting in the car next to Sastro. With a quick motion of the steering wheel he suddenly avoided a cat crossing the road. In answer to my complimentary remarks he said that he always looked out very carefully for cats. If you ran over and killed a cat, he told me, the Prophet, who was a cat lover, would punish you: before being allowed to enter Paradise you would first have to count every hair of the animal. That's why even today I always slow down a bit when I see a cat on the street as I'm driving, just to be sure.

Sometimes it happened that the servants would be away for a few days. That was *lebaran,* the end of the fast, celebrated with festive meals, visits to relatives, and the purchase of new clothes. It always announced itself the same way: the servants would ask for a few days off so they could go back to their native village. They always asked for an advance as well.

I never noticed much of the fasting period—Ramadan—or of the other manifestations of Islam. On the island of Java, Islam was, and still is, a thin layer of religious veneer on a substratum of traditional animism and Hindu customs. In any event, in the cities it played a very small role in the population's everyday life. In 1892 Snouck Hurgronje[5] wrote that in the Dutch East Indies the only one able to recite flawless Arabic was the mynah bird in his cage in the back of the yard. The mynah bird is an amazing imitator of the human voice.

At night, when our parents were at the club and it was quiet in the house, the *babu* would watch us. Talking in a low whisper, she'd sit in the rear gallery with a woman friend or a niece beside her on a mat of woven bamboo by the light of a little oil lamp and watch over us until our parents came home. If it became very late—and that was not unusual—she'd sleep right there in the gallery. To reach the toilet we had to go through several rooms and then down the long, covered walkway. It was comforting to see her sleeping figure in the faint light of the rear gallery, because at night we thought the trek "to the back" was a little creepy. On the walls of the rooms there were dozens of *cicaks,* motionless little

---

5. Snouck Hurgronje (1857–1936) was a world-famous Dutch Arabist.

lizards that would suddenly dart off in pursuit of a mosquito. They could drop to the ground abruptly with a soft, moist, smacking sound. In the hallway you'd be on the alert for the large, shiny black beetles that whirred through the night and with a dull thud of their armored shield occasionally hit against something.

There was often a *tauke,* a gecko, on a crossbeam, a little horned-combed dragon about twenty centimeters long. I didn't dare pass by it on my own, although the little creature never did anything. When the babu had accompanied me to the toilet, she'd lead me back, put me beside her on the mat and pull me close, saying: "Listen carefully, when he calls his name seven times you can make a wish." And we'd listen to his call *tauke, tauke, tauke.* I'd fall asleep surrounded by her scent of soap, coconut oil, and *sirih,* betel.

My parents went to the club all the time. It was a large, white building with ballrooms, billiard rooms, and bars. In the vast shaded garden a dance floor was laid out in the open air, an egg-shaped plateau of pink marble. At children's parties we were allowed to roller-skate there, but at night it was the adults' hunting ground.

Late one night I was permitted to go along with our driver who'd been asked to pick up my parents after a reception or some festive gathering. Other drivers were also waiting behind the gate for their *tuans* and *nyonyas,* their masters and mistresses.

With lots of loud laughter and talk the party was in full swing. Chanting and drinking songs resounded. A more or less sublimated decadence reigned supreme. On the dance floor, right out in the open, there was some genuine necking and petting: the tuans and nyonyas did just about anything other than actually copulate.

Sitting on their haunches behind the gate, the drivers watched. Their faces showed no expression. I was sitting next to them and all of a sudden looking at what the adult Europeans were up to through their eyes. Even now that memory still causes me a slight discomfort.

Often their entertainment wasn't limited to the club. Many Europeans were in the habit of having one for the road in a less formal atmosphere. Somewhere "downtown" in the old Batavia area where no decent person lived anymore there was a nightclub, The Black Cat.

My mother had a gift for frivolity, and years later when we had long been back in Holland, she could still tell us with great animation about this place of amusement and its patrons.

In contrast to the club, at The Black Cat there was no question of any discrimination. The public consisted of indigenous night owls, Chinese gangsters, seedy Europeans, and down-and-out KNIL deserters. There were Japanese proprietors of hair salons and photo studios as well. They were neither hairdressers nor photographers but spies of the emperor of Nippon. Frequently there were U-boat officers of the German Kriegsmarine as well, who were not sailors at all but hydrologists, oceanographers, or meteorologists mapping out the Indian Ocean as the future area of operations for their führer. The public would dance deep into the night, not on a marble floor but on the tables. No sophisticated cocktails were served but a nasty arak instead, the strong native rice brandy, or else absinthe, the "green fairy," a forbidden and dangerous beverage. Those present devoted themselves wholeheartedly to activities that in the USA were known as "making whoopee."

Even though our parents didn't actually prohibit me and my friends from making a trip to the pasar, it still had the appeal of something that wasn't really allowed.

We'd head there on afternoons off from school to look at all the commotion and the hubbub. We wandered around between the baskets of fruit and vegetables and the many stands. Market people were different from the servants. The men were more detached, and the women much less mild-mannered than the babu and the koki. If for just a split second you were in the way, you'd get a hard push from an elbow or a knee.

We'd drink the sickly sweet, ice-cold pink lemonade with crushed ice that was always served in very thick glasses. We loved it, mostly because our parents had explicitly forbidden it, saying it was "dirty."

There were piles of sticky fruit, meat covered with flies, and dried fish that smelled of rot and decay. Hundreds of little birds fluttered around in cages, live chickens were hanging by their feet from poles, and ducks were crammed together in straw baskets. Blacksmiths, bicycle repairmen, hairdressers, and writers were at work. Most of the small shops along the road of the marketplace were run by fat, worried-looking Chinese. They sat inside their stores chock-full of cans, barrels, and canvas bags with groceries, dried red and green peppers, all sorts of beans and peas, packages of matches, and brightly colored candy in apothecary jars. Their sons were calm, robust boys. We never saw them at play. They were always working for their fathers. We'd imitate the high-pitched sounds of their language, and to tease them we'd sometimes toss stones inside, which would clatter against the glass and the tin cans. They tolerated this so stoically that we soon gave up.

There were "Bombayans" at the pasar as well. That is what the textile merchants were called who commonly came from the city of Bombay in British India. These were tall men with beards and heads bound in turbans. They wore their shirts hanging loosely over their pants. They'd sit amid large stacks and rolls of light blue, green, and pink fabric. They were quite friendly.

Other people I encountered were dogcatchers and coolies.

One day I saw a small yellowish dog roaming around our neighborhood, staggering and disoriented, adrift on the now completely abandoned street. He was rabid. His brains were already almost entirely consumed by the blind madness, and his head was drooping halfway down. His body was moving back and forth as if trying to shake something off.

I was watching from the garden. My mother called me from the terrace to come inside. The scene fascinated me, so I pretended not to hear her. Then I felt the kebun's arms around me, lifting me up in one quick motion and carrying me inside.

The dogcatcher and his cronies chased after rabid and other stray dogs. Their van was one part cage, one part closed bin in which dogs that had a tag were locked up and later returned to their owners. Stray dogs were usually thin as a rake and mangy. They were hunted down and routinely trapped in a dead-end alley where they were bludgeoned to death. In the cage the remaining dogs would yelp and bark.

The street coolies worked on the roadside. They were manual laborers, anonymous people dressed in rags, a frayed pair of pants and occasionally a shirt full of holes. They reeked of sweat. These were rough men, untouchables of a sort. You didn't address them, and they didn't speak to you. Their eyes were dull, their proletarian poverty emitted a vague threat. Often you'd choose to walk on the other side of the street.

Behind our house was an area with small narrow streets, low houses, and little yards where Eurasian clerks and functionaries lived. These were simple people with very modest incomes and many sons and daughters.

All the Eurasian boys in the neighborhood owned pigeons, and sometimes they'd briefly let us hold one of them. When you tightly clasped the wings and little feet, the warm, small, blue-gray body fit right inside your hand. It was a blissful sensation that I only recognized many years later when I caressed my first girlfriend.

Competitions were organized. In a basket on the back of his bike one of the boys would take the pigeons some distance away and then let them fly off. Holding the females, the other boys waited. A small, colorfully painted clay flute was attached between the pigeons' tail feathers. Each flute had its own sound by which the owner recognized his bird. The wait came to an end when the frail sound of the little flutes announced the appearance of the pigeons. When the birds were sighted high in the sky, the boys would beckon them home by lifting up the females they were holding and letting them flap their wings. The males would then rush down from way up high while the sound of the flutes grew louder and louder. Whoever had a pigeon land on his arm first was the winner. I don't think I ever watched a more exciting spectacle.

The war was approaching, but my friends and I weren't particularly concerned. We eagerly accepted the public opinion assuring us that the Japanese weren't able to fly because they were much too bow-legged and because they all wore glasses. Besides, they flew inferior imitation planes, so it was said.

The adults should have known better. Japan had already been waging war in China with the most modern technical materials. The attack on Pearl Harbor in December 1941 may well have been morally and diplomatically reprehensible, but technically, organizationally, and logistically it was indisputably a brilliant operation. Many years later I read that, as early as 1940, American professional journals stated in no uncertain terms that the Japanese fighter plane, the Zero, was of superior quality. Of course, I didn't read that journal in 1940, but apparently neither did many high-ranking people. I let myself be swept along by that self-satisfied Western hubris, but for the rest of my life I knew this: *never* underestimate your adversary.

Despite this lightheartedness, here and there preparations for war were nevertheless made. Many people had an "air-raid shelter" built in their yard. As did my parents. It was a two-meter-deep trench, covered with a roof made of *atap,* dried palm leaves, and one went down into it by a bamboo ladder. Within two weeks it was filled with half a meter of water, and the walls began to cave in. Rats and other vermin quickly found a home there. The absolute, almost surrealistic uselessness of this shelter soon became obvious to me, as it did to everyone else. The strange thing is that I never for a moment doubted my father's acumen.

Here and there throughout Batavia were kiosks run by Indonesian merchants. They sold newspapers, lemonade, and sweets. Late one afternoon at the end of February 1942 I was biking home from the Cikini swimming pool with my friend Rick. He had some change on him, and we decided to buy candy in one of the kiosks. Seated behind the window, wearing a round black headcover and a fine shirt, the salesman was reading a paper.

We made our choice, and Rick put the money on the counter and asked the man, who was looking for change, what time it was. He addressed him with *kwee,* a Malay second person form that has a pejorative undertone and emphasizes the inferiority of the one addressed. For several moments the man looked at him without saying a word.

"Kwee?" he said. "What kwee? This is kwee." And he pointed at some sweet cookies that in Malay are also known as kwee. He flung the change on the counter, and while he looked fixedly at the ground, his slow underhanded gesture made us leave very fast.

Two weeks later the Japanese troops landed on the coast of West Java. That was the moment when the Fates changed horses, and the world of the Dutch East Indies became history.

Chapter 5

BATAVIA, OPEN CITY

One day in March 1942 we were sitting on our terrace, as always at the end of the day. My father wasn't there. He had left a few weeks earlier to accompany the governor-general and his staff to the Bandung garrison because they thought that city was easier to defend. I don't remember his departure at all, probably because everyone thought it would be only temporary; after all, the Allies would win the war within a month or two. We were not to see my father again for another three and a half years.

Aunt Nancy was there. She was one of my great-aunts and had just been widowed a month before, so my mother had invited her to come and stay with us for a while.

We were drinking tea. The street was quiet. No traffic, just an occasional pedestrian passing by. Batavia had been declared an "open city," and the defenseless town was holding its breath, awaiting the arrival of the Japanese troops.

"There's one," my mother suddenly said in a quiet agitated tone. A slightly stooped Japanese soldier was walking in the dry bed of the ditch across the street. He carried his long rifle in front of him with the bayonet pointing upward at a slant. He wasn't wearing a helmet but a cotton fighter's cap with a cloth at the back covering his neck to protect it from the sun. The KNIL soldiers we knew were always loaded down with a backpack, cartridge boxes, a water bottle, and small tin pans. But this Japanese soldier wasn't hampered by a backpack or hip packs at his belt, which gave him a lithe and nimble look. His uniform was a yellowish olive green and hung loosely around his body. The fabric looked cheap. He didn't look up, completely ignoring us. Just past our house he was suddenly approached by a local man who said something to him. He was welcoming the soldier, I assume, for at first the indigenous population treated the Japanese quite positively.

Without a moment's hesitation, however, the Japanese soldier struck the man with his open hand, a rapid blow in the face, and then continued on his way as if nothing had happened. "Asia for the Asians, as you can see," Aunt Nancy said, not without a certain satisfaction.

That same afternoon my mother ordered the servants to pour all alcoholic beverages—and there was quite a bit—down the garden drain. That's what the authorities had advised on the radio, keeping in mind the scenes that had played out in various Chinese cities after the Japanese troops invaded them. In Batavia a fortune must have gone down the drain because the colonial community wasn't exactly known for its moderation or self-denial.

A few days later Japanese soldiers were billeted in the school across the street from us. Several officers moved into a vacant house next to ours. When they came home after being on duty in the afternoon they politely greeted my mother, and shortly thereafter, just like us, they'd be sitting on the terrace in front of their house. Eating raw fish, as my Aunt Nancy used to observe with loathing. One of them played the piano a lot, always European composers: Chopin, Schubert, or Mozart. "I have to admit, they do have fine taste in music," my mother said somewhat reluctantly.

Guards stood in front of the school gate. The first few days we were afraid to ride our bikes past them, but it soon turned out there was no reason to be scared. They didn't bother us. After a few more days we were told that we had to greet the guards with a bow. My mother and the other women were highly indignant about that. "Just think *lousy Jap* while you bow," they said, but we got used to it pretty quickly, and it didn't really worry us.

As mentioned, among the adults the obligation to bow to the Japanese military aroused great resentment. The Europeans felt it as a deliberate humiliation. But anyone familiar with Japanese culture knows it is very normal for the Japanese, a gesture of good manners that has a completely different meaning than it does for us. Furthermore, by Japanese standards there wasn't really that much demanded of us. We weren't required to stand at rigid attention or bow three or four times in a row. The children failed to notice the clash of cultures completely. It was something that only the adults got excited about. When a Japanese soldier came close, we interrupted our play and did what we were expected to do.

Once in a great while the Japanese soldiers would beckon to be photographed together with us. We'd all be laughing. I suspect that I was placed on the sideboard of many a Japanese home as a fortunate participant in the "Greater East Asian Prosperity Sphere," as the Japanese called their conquests.

Once a guard let my sister and me ride by on our bicycles, motioning us to keep moving without bowing. Apparently, he wasn't in the mood for the ritual because they did have to return the greeting. But he would regret it, as an officer who just at that moment was leaving the school saw what happened. We knew him: he lived next door to us; he was the one who played the piano. Irate, he blew up at the poor guard and dragged him into the school building. We watched them both enter the courtyard. The officer beat the soldier on the head from behind with his fists and kicked him in the side with his boots.

In the afternoon the soldiers regularly trained in the field next to the school. They practiced bayonet fighting and, roaring loudly, pierced straw pallets with their bayonet. Other times they had to wrestle each other, for which they'd rub their entire body with oil. On that occasion all they wore were small white loincloths, tied like a diaper with a belt around their middle. We sat on the terrace and watched. "Barbarians," Aunt Nancy whispered, but for me it had a certain fascination. I actually found it rather tough.

When evening fell, other platoons returned from marching drill. They would sing marvelous songs that even now sometimes run through my head at night.

In those days my friends and I would go to the Cikini swimming pool every day after school. One day I came home around six. The street was empty, the school deserted, the driveway swept clean, the gravel raked, the Japanese soldiers gone. Our neighbors, too, had left. I thought it was pretty boring.

During the first few months of the occupation many inhabitants abandoned their homes. Families moved in with each other for security; some women had followed their husbands when these were unexpectedly transferred. Occasionally we boys would explore such abandoned homes. More often than not looters, *rampokkers,* had preceded us, leaving the houses not so much robbed clean as totally ravaged. Windows smashed, faucets and water pipes ripped out of the wall, pillows and mattresses torn open and shaken out. The corners of the rooms showed burns and singed spots, and the floor was littered with shards and paper shreds. Sometimes we found the bloated cadaver of a cat or a large pile of poop teeming with white maggots that lay in the middle of a room. A sinister atmosphere of destructive rage filled these homes. It was both creepy and exciting. Those coolies in their threadbare rags with their big feet and wide-spread toes were here, I thought.

In my recollection the first weeks of the Japanese occupation passed by quite calmly. The invading army conducted itself with discipline. In Batavia they distributed the telephone number of a Japanese police department that one could call to complain if one suffered any harassment. Rampokkers caught in the act were summarily shot.

For the adult Europeans these were undoubtedly frightening and uncertain times, but the children didn't pay it much heed.

Chapter 6

KRAMAT

In Batavia the internment started in late October 1942. The first snow had already fallen in Stalingrad. Strangely enough, this news was broadcast in great detail, although the radio was entirely controlled by the Japanese. My mother would listen intently and said that this was good news because the Germans were going to have a very hard time of it. She couldn't have heard it via a foreign station because our radio set was sealed in such a way that only those stations approved by the Japanese authorities could be received. And my mother wasn't so much courageous as she was technically too inept to mess around with the seal.

For a brief time, when the internment was announced, a peculiar movement was created among the European population. It was made public that people with Indonesian blood didn't have to enter the camps. Consequently, some women went searching assiduously for proof of a mixed origin. Indonesian or indigenous ancestors magically appeared by legitimate means or not, such as bribing the functionaries at the county clerk's office. "It always concerns the ancestry of a Balinese princess and a Westphalian count, never of a Swiss charcoal carrier and a *ronggeng,* a dancing girl from Tasikmalaya," my mother scornfully remarked.

Moreover, in the course of 1942 the urban mood of the indigenous population had grown more hostile toward the Europeans. Thus, the internment camp offered a kind of protection as well.

The Japanese called it *tempat perlindungan,* a protective area, which wasn't entirely inaccurate.

As we now know, protecting the Europeans was not the true motive of the Japanese authorities. It was the beginning of an unswerving policy aimed at isolating the Western influences and ultimately eliminating them. They would be very successful at it.

The camp was called Kramat, after the neighborhood where it was located. We were put up in a small house on the Laan Wychert Kecil, which means Little Laan Wychert, a side street of the large Laan Wychert. At first it wasn't really a camp yet but part of the district designated to house European women and children.

At the time the Kramat district was located on the edge of the city. It was a nineteenth-century, typical Indies *tempo dulu* neighborhood, an area of the past, with spacious colonial homes, all of them surrounded by vast gardens. The streets and avenues were shaded by majestic *kenari,* Javanese almond trees, which with a clatter would drop tasty nuts on the asphalt when the wind blew. Initially, the district wasn't fenced off at all, but after a few months a bamboo enclosure rose up, and the camp acquired an actual gate with a guard. We had been forced to abandon the radio but were allowed to bring along furniture, linens, and kitchen equipment. The first few months the Dutch ladies were permitted to keep babus, female house-servants, in their service so that initially their lives didn't change all that much: the servants did the household work, and the nyonyas, the ladies, kept themselves busy with visiting each other, having tea, making music, and playing bridge. The babus arrived at the camp early in the morning, cheerfully chattering.

On the west side the camp's boundary was formed by the broad and brown Ciliwung River that flowed through Batavia to the sea. There was no fence or other separation. On the other side of the river naked indigenous children played in the water near the bank. There was a large urban village that three years later was to become the shelter of the *pemudas,* the young fanatic freedom fighters of the revolution.

Because the camp commanders usually placed two or three families in one house, we had less space than we did before the war. But the homes certainly weren't overcrowded yet as they would be later on.

There were few adult men in the camp. They had been locked up earlier in men's camps and prisons. My mother received monthly checks, payments that were sent from the prisoner of war camp in Batavia where, as it turned out, my father was incarcerated. The check was always signed by a certain Lieutenant Sone Kenichi, a name that at the time meant nothing to us. Later on, in the course of 1943, these remittances stopped abruptly without any further announcement or explanation. If my mother ever received any letters from or other news about my father, I never heard about it.

For the children it was a carefree time. There was no danger, and we weren't hungry in the least. Japanese soldiers would suddenly enter the camp at random under the command of an officer. They'd search the houses for concealed radios and in the process were anything but gentle; closets were roughly opened and emptied out, furniture and beds were irritably shoved aside, but they never touched any children.

I was nine years old but still remember those house searches very clearly. Most of the women reacted with fear, servility, or condescension. My mother remained calm, looked the soldiers evenly in the eyes, and without a trace of arrogance replied in a businesslike but polite tone to the questions that the accompanying local policemen posed.

I saw the Japanese officer, who was standing by with arms crossed, closely watching my mother. It didn't escape me that he was evaluating her behavior and appreciating it. He saw that I saw it, and when he left he gave me an almost imperceptible approving little nod. I was proud of her. She was thirty-four then. It wasn't the last time that I was aware of her even-tempered tranquil courage.

We children played in the camp's broad avenues: roller skates, marbles, the exciting game of *kasti,* a kind of softball, and making fires. Without any traffic in the street the world was all ours. What was annoying was that the mothers had organized schoolwork after only a few days. Later the Japanese authorities prohibited this altogether, of which we heartily approved.

Until June 1943 we were allowed to leave the internment camp on Sundays. They gave you an ID card, and then you could go downtown for shopping or to the hairdresser. One Sunday in March 1943, my mother took us to a Chinese photographer to have a portrait taken of herself, my sister, and me. Many people used the occasion as an outing to visit friends or relatives who remained outside the camp. All of a sudden having indigenous family was very convenient.

That is how I came to know Uncle Jan, a Eurasian cousin of my father's. He was a very Indonesian man, almost entirely "gone native," as they used to call it then. He lived in an area of Batavia where previously we would never go. It was a crowded popular district filled with little stone dwellings, alternating with village huts and now and then a *big* house. Uncle Jan was a very simple, very nice man who ran a shabby bicycle shop with an adjoining workplace, a true *bengkel,* a little repair shed. As far as I know there had been no contact before the war between this man and my parents, but on the Sundays that we were free to go he warmly welcomed my mother and her two children into his extremely simple surroundings. He lived with his Indonesian wife, who spoke not one word of Dutch, in a "pavilion," as the small, freestanding abodes were called, often situated on the edge of the yard of a big residence. Originally they were intended for transient people and houseguests, a practical facility that went back to the nineteenth century. Normally they comprised nothing more than two rooms and a small rear gallery.

A Bombayan and his family lived in the big house to which his lodging belonged, a British Indian textile merchant from whom Uncle Jan rented the pavilion. "A true gentleman," my mother remarked in a tone of slight surprise. He always had *splendid news* about the battle in Tunis and the actions of the American Navy in

My mother, sister, and I. The photo was taken in a Chinese photography shop on a Sunday in March 1943. Until June 1943, we were allowed to leave Kramat Camp on Sundays. Notice that I am wearing shoes. Notice also the cloth band on my mother's right arm, indicating that she had permission to be outside the camp.

the Pacific. "The warrr is almost overrr," he would say. The way he spoke and his quiet bearing enthralled me. I was familiar with his compatriots from the market, but here he was different; here he was more invulnerable, less servile, more himself, as it were.

Camp Kramat was vacated a few months later, and the continual merging of the internment camps began, which to the exasperation of the women the Japanese authorities would continue throughout the war. The camps became smaller and more crowded.

In September 1943, in a long parade of jauntily clanging pedicabs, *becaks,* we were transported to Camp Cideng. We weren't allowed to bring furniture and similar items; only bed linen was permitted. And that turned out to be a good thing because Cideng had far less space.

I never saw Uncle Jan again, never heard anything about him either. I don't know how, or if, he weathered the storm of war and revolution. To some extent I hold it against my parents that, as far as I know, after August 1945 they never worried about him anymore. Maybe it was impossible at the time. I hope that fate rewarded him for his kindness and concern for us and that he and his family were safely absorbed into the population. But I wish I could be sure.

Chapter 7

CIDENG

Cideng, the women's internment camp, was located in a different part of Batavia, on the city's west side along the railroad that was separated from the residential area by a deep and fairly wide waterway. On the other side of the tracks was an open field with paddies and fishponds. The district had been constructed more recently than Kramat. The houses and gardens were smaller, more European, and the stately avenues were missing. Other than that, life wasn't half bad, at least when I was there. We no longer had servants; they weren't allowed to enter the camps anymore. Perhaps that was annoying for the women, but we didn't care. Until the middle of 1944 people had dogs and cats in the camp as pets until the Japanese camp command no longer permitted that either. The money transfers to my mother had been stopped, which wasn't really a disaster because the Japanese authorities had food delivered to the gate every day. My mother earned money by making and selling candy. She was able to order the necessary sugar and fruit from the outside. At the time money was therefore still circulating among the incarcerated women.

The camp was already quite crowded with many women and children. We were living with about fifteen people in a house built for a single European family. Each woman occupied one room together with her children. Later, the camp would grow even more congested.

The children played in the street all day long. We would play hopscotch and marbles, and roller-skate on the wide asphalt of Trivelli Avenue. We were avid players of a native street game whose name I have forgotten, for which you needed one long stick, one short stick, and two flat stones, but I clearly remember the rules of the game and how to keep score. We made huts in the trees and played cowboys and Indians with homemade bows and arrows. We built small carts from the undercarriages of baby strollers, with which we held races or contests of skill in the Musi Road. Plenty of space.

We caught praying mantises in the trees and bushes and kept them in bamboo cages. These were impassive, fluorescent green insects whose front paws had hinged barbs that they used to hold their prey—other insects—in a merciless grip. We were captivated how during their mating the female used to grab the male by its head and then eat him. We founded clubs we called The Secret Club or The Black Panther, of which you couldn't just automatically become a member. We even turned the camp's daily roll call into a game. For this, the entire camp population had to gather in part of the street near the gate. When the count was done, we'd run home as fast as we could straight across front yards and through holes in the hedges and fences. Whoever was first to sit on the stoop of the house was the winner.

In the rainy season we played Game of the Goose or Monopoly, but more often than not we were bored stiff indoors.

It was a carefree time for us. A continuous vacation: there was no school, which was strictly forbidden, and that suited me fine. Attending school before the war hadn't agreed with me. Because of the many times we had moved during the last three years, I had changed schools frequently and every time had to get used to a new teacher and, as the newcomer, try to integrate into the group of other boys. I was an active child and didn't like sitting still. Once my mother asked me what I liked best at school, and, to her amusement, I answered "recess." Now I could play outside all day long.

In April 1944 all the civilian camps were placed under the direct control of the army. From that moment on they were known officially as military internment camps.

A few weeks later the circumstances in the camps began to grow gradually worse. "The friendliness of the Japs has ended," the women said. The economist Kondo, one of the civil functionaries who had come along as administrators in the service of the Japanese occupying army, was replaced as camp commander by a military officer.

There still was plenty to eat in the camp. On 15 May 1944 my mother wrote in her diary: "Where food is concerned we are doing marvelously! In addition to cornmeal and rice Nippon now also gives us brown beans, *kacang hijau* [mung beans], gula jawa, candy, and soap. Meat or fish almost every day! An egg every fourth day. Not much fruit or leafy vegetables though."

It was wartime, but we didn't notice it all that much.

"Camp life is paradise for Freddy," my mother noted in her diary around the same period.

We had to perform duties but didn't mind because it was manly. Actually, we had to construct the fence around the camp. Rock-solid poles were embedded into the ground every few meters, and these were joined with lattices on which we'd nail the *gedek,* mats of woven bamboo. The youth from the kampung on the other side of the tracks shouted and sneered and enriched our repertoire of vulgar curse words and expressions, all of which I have unfortunately forgotten.

In his book about Cideng, *Bezonken rood* (*Sunken Red*), Jeroen Brouwers mentions barbed wire, watchtowers, searchlights, and machine guns—images that created quite a furor. This is nonsense, as I know from experience. After all, I made the fence myself. Indeed, in pictures of that fence taken a few days after the capitulation in August 1945, all you see is a rather flimsy enclosure.

Also manly but much less fun was doing sentry duty. This occurred at night, and its purpose was protecting the camp from outside thieves—native people, in other words—who would climb over the fence looking for fabric hanging on the laundry lines. Apparently, by then the lack of cloth had already increased enormously among the Javanese urban population.

When you saw their shadows slip through the yards, you'd hit a stone against an iron lamppost as hard as you could to alert your buddies and ask them for help. I can still hear that sound. God, how scared I was, more scared than I ever was of any "Jap."

Usually, like everyone else, we would rest in the afternoon when it was hottest. My mother, my sister Carolien, and I lived together in the small front room of a house on the Citarum Road, far from the main gate. It was a nice part of the day, quiet and calm. We'd doze off or read or chat about daily events or about the war. My mother was a realist. "You shouldn't believe all those rumors about the Americans already being in Surabaya and that sort of thing," she said. "The war is going to go on for a long time yet."

"And life will never be the way it was before," she would add. "What will it be like then?" I asked, somewhat shocked, for I was really counting on living on the Sunda Road again with all the familiar servants and the cats. "I really don't know," she'd say matter-of-factly. "We'll just have to see."

An exemplary attitude.

One day in May 1944 we were in bed, and my mother was reading to us from Jules Verne's *Twenty Thousand Leagues under the Sea*. Suddenly we heard footsteps in the street, loud footsteps that soon crunched on the gravel in the yard. All of a sudden there was a Japanese officer in the room. It was the new commander, Lieutenant Sone. Startled, we scrambled to our feet, bowed, not quite knowing what to do. He returned the bow. "Lanzing?" he asked. He pronounced it *Lang Sing*. "Yes," my mother said. I was standing next to her a little sheepishly, not daring to look at him. After all, you weren't face to face with a Japanese officer all that often. He was wearing black boots. His green uniform fit him well and wasn't made of the same cheap material as what the Japanese soldiers were made to wear. He was tall for a Japanese, with a slender athletic build. He looked me up and down, his hands on his hips, then nodded a few times. "Son, yes," he said as he continued looking at me. He turned around abruptly without a word and was gone.

A few days later he came back again, just as unexpectedly as the first time. "Your husband is well," he said to my mother. He looked at me at length again. "Your son?" he asked once more. "Yes," my mother answered. He motioned for me to follow him and left the yard, into the street. The asphalt under my bare feet was hot. He was taking long strides, and every now and then I had to start trotting to keep up with him. We walked between bowing women whom I heard whispering my name as we passed. I felt quite ill at ease.

He lived in a large house just outside the camp's gate where Trivelli Avenue and the Cideng waterway intersected. We went in. He indicated that I should sit down and then disappeared. I wasn't afraid, but I was confused and felt a bit uneasy. A short while later he returned with a bucket of warm water, little jars of ointment, and a roll of gauze dressing. He carefully washed my feet and rubbed some pink ointment on the two tropical ulcers I had on one toe and the heel of my right foot that simply wouldn't heal. It wasn't all that strange because I hadn't worn any shoes for a very long time. In addition to the ulcers, the bottom of each foot had grown a thick layer of calluses. My feet had become so tough that I could tie metal roller skates onto my bare skin without any pain or discomfort.

He placed a piece of gauze on the wounds and rolled the bandage around my foot. He was kneeling in front of me and said nothing. He had two stars on his lapels. His hair was cropped very close. His head was large and round. I saw his face close up. He was very focused on what he was doing. He had a regular Japanese face with fairly thick eyebrows, large brown eyes, a straight nose, and full lips. I could even smell him. He had that odd odor that apparently originates in the Japanese diet. When Sone was done, he got up, gave me a banana, and said something in Japanese. I nodded, but of course I had no clue. He repeated his words. I nodded again. He said something else and motioned with his hand. I understood that he was sending me away and walked back into the camp with the snow-white bandage around my foot.

Two weeks later he came back to the house to get me. He pointed at my foot, shook his head, and said something in a soft, half-chastising tone. Of course, his treatment hadn't done any good. The bandage was long gone, and the wounds looked just as they had before. I couldn't think of anything better to do than shrug my shoulders. Again he bandaged my foot, and this time gave me a glass of ice water, something I hadn't tasted in a very long time!

Sone ran a harsh and volatile regime in Cideng. He lived right near the camp together with his Eurasian woman friend. He was actively involved in how things were run, which was extraordinary: most Japanese camp commanding officers rarely showed their faces. But Sone appeared in the camp with great regularity. He terrorized the women with his ferocious explosions of rage about trivialities. Once I saw him burst into a fury about a camp number that had been pinned askew onto someone's blouse. He beat the woman violently on the head. He went especially berserk when the moon was full, a literal lunacy that was notorious.

The women and children often sat outside on nights of the full moon to enjoy the quiet, cool night. The light was so bright that you could read by it. And then it would begin. First you'd hear cursing and howling and the loud banging of objects falling over. Then in the glassy moonlight you'd see his figure come closer, like a wandering demon, robbed of his senses, and everyone would rush inside.

He had the habit of making the women and children move incessantly, and the camp grew ever smaller, with more and more people being housed there. Sometimes he imposed collective punishment on the entire camp, in the form of an extra roll call, for example, when food had been smuggled in across the fence. Such roll calls could last for hours and were a true ordeal for everyone. These punitive actions weren't limited to

The house of Captain Sone Kenichi at the entrance of Cideng Camp, situated at the corner of the Cideng Canal and Trivelli Avenue. The house was demolished sometime after the war.

the internees, however. He severely punished four indigenous soldiers who, according to him, had been too accommodating during a roll call. They were punched in the face for everyone to see. Consequently, his subordinates were quite afraid of him and sometimes collaborated secretly with the women so as not to arouse his ire. Thus it would happen that the guard at the gate might alert the women with a hand motion that the commander was about to enter the camp.

The following weeks he came to pick me up every now and then, too. At first I felt rather uncomfortable, but I was never scared. His look was kind, and his hands were gentle. In the way I came to know him at those moments he did not resemble the cruel commander at all. It was as if he had two personalities. Most of the time he took care of my feet, even though he must have realized it was a fairly pointless undertaking. He always gave me some fruit, but, beyond that, I wasn't given any preferential treatment or other privileges. It never lasted very long. He'd wash my feet, rub ointment on the wounds, and wrap a clean bandage around my foot.

One time he didn't send me away after taking care of my foot but instead pointed to a seat on the terrace. Several officers, colleagues of his, were coming to visit. They drank tea. At the outset they'd address me now and then, but then they became involved in their own conversation, and I had the feeling they'd forgotten about me. Sitting on a straight-backed chair, I just wanted it to be over. When the visitors left hours later, I was allowed to go as well.

Fortunately, that was the only time, and I hadn't liked it at all.

As far as I know, I was his only pet. I accepted his care and attention without giving it much thought and without becoming immersed in his motivations. I never discussed it with my mother, not even after the war. And no one else ever commented on it.

For the last ten months of Sone's regime in Cideng we weren't there any longer.

My mother, Carolien, and I were transferred to a different camp, just outside of Batavia, at the end of October 1944. We were told that it was a punitive measure, but my mother never did find out why she was being punished.

Sone lost sight of me. At least, so I thought.

Chapter 8

TANGERANG

We were transferred to the Juvenile Correctional Institute in Tangerang, a small town just outside of Batavia. The institution had been built to keep people locked up, a real prison. It was a square building that had a large tiled inner courtyard with the central kitchen in the middle. On all sides in a square around the courtyard were dormitories, spacious areas for bathing, and elongated latrines you crouched above, which stayed clean because the water flowed through them continuously. Faucets everywhere provided water at any time of day. We weren't used to this anymore, for in Cideng there had always been a water shortage.

It was a prison, but at least it had the advantage of being designed to shelter large numbers of inmates without causing problems of hygiene or accommodation. There were fields around the building for the cultivation of vegetables and fruit by and for the inhabitants. Behind the building was a large yard with lawns and tall kapok trees that provided lots of shade. If there was any surveillance at all, it was practically invisible. No Japanese ever entered the institution.

I hated it there. Three stern ladies ruled the boys' dormitory, where they established a regime that still recurs regularly in my nightmares. They imposed a daily schedule on us, full of Boy Scout ceremonies, songs, and forced merriment. In the morning we were made to do all kinds of unpleasant chores: clear drainage pipes, stack up wood for the kitchens, collect garbage and toss it in a foul-smelling dumping site just outside the institution. In the afternoon we had to set up our own vegetable gardens under the building's walls. It wasn't so much the work that we couldn't stand; what was much worse was that they always broke us up into teams to compete in neatness or speed. For this we won points, which we were supposed to enjoy.

It was my first and last experience with a totalitarian regime that controlled our life every minute of the day.

It began as soon as we got up: a loud whistle at the sound of which you had to immediately stand beside your bed. Then, your head still sluggish, you had to sing a "cheerful" morning song, after which they marched you off to the shower rooms. Everything on command: soaping ("down below as well!"), drying off (but if you took a little too long "down below" you got a hard smack on your arm). We were lined up for literally everything. We couldn't go anywhere spontaneous; we were always marched off, and then had to sing a song or suddenly exclaim: "We're doing our best." All day long. You had the feeling you were constantly being watched, no way to make a bit of a racket every now and then. You always had to stand straight, "like one of Jan de Witt's boys."[6] And woe be upon you if you kept your hands in your pockets. "A healthy Dutch boy wouldn't dream of doing that." Their obsessive preoccupation with "cleanliness" drew our attention to "it" all the more. Behind the ladies' backs you'd grimace and vigorously scratch your scrotum.

Throughout the day they'd set you up in a false comradeship against each other with competitions in virtue, virtue in things over which you had absolutely no power: "Whose tomato plant grew most during the night?" It still makes me angry.

Sometimes we had time off. God, how we loved that.

Fortunately, some two months later, in early January, I turned twelve and that officially made me a *prisoner of war*. It rather suited me, and I was even a little proud of it. At the time

---

6. The expression probably originated with J(oh)an de Witt, perhaps the most important seventeenth-century Dutch politician, who was assassinated together with his brother Cornelis in August 1672. His "boys" were strong, brave, and fearless.

I wasn't aware how extremely fortunate it was that we had been sent to a boys' camp and not to a real prisoner of war camp, for the prisoners in most of the POW camps were forced to do hard labor under tough command.

About transferring boys from women's to men's camps much has been written, and always with great resentment.

Not surprisingly, my turn came in January 1945. It was common knowledge that twelve-year-old boys were periodically relocated. I didn't mind it in the least. In the women's camp the atmosphere was oppressive, and the other kids and I didn't quite know how to handle that. Many of the internees were young women and pubescent girls. They often wore shorts, so that you could clearly see their thighs, and something like a bodice on top, a cloth tied around the neck and the waist covering the bust but leaving the back bare. We soon discovered the old truth that clothes frequently highlight what they conceal more than what remains visible. And we were reaching an age where you love to look at women and girls all the time and then want to touch and scrutinize them further.

We were being treated as children, and we took advantage of it when it suited us. Putting on an angelic face, we'd accompany our mothers on free afternoons to the bathing space full of naked women and girls. When we were together at night, alone in the dormitory, we'd report excitedly on all the female shapes and forms in every stage of flowering and decay. "*Aduh,* oh boy," Kees said. "I quickly had to wrap a towel around me!" And we laughed and had fun. Some of the boys had discovered masturbation. "I ejaculated," one boy called out one quiet night. Others claimed that a young widow had done "it" with them.

And so, one afternoon in January 1945, I was driven out of Camp Tangerang together with another dozen boys my age in an open truck guarded by two drenched *heihos,* Indonesian military aides. I breathed a sigh of relief: away from Tangerang, away from the clutches of the den mothers. It was raining cats and dogs, and my sister was crying her eyes out. My mother was wise enough not to load me down with all sorts of good advice, nor did she weep pitifully as did so many other mothers. She calmly said good-bye in a way that didn't embarrass me.

First the truck went to an assembly point in Batavia, which turned out to be Camp Cideng. We were driven as far as the gate. Soaking wet and chilled to the bone, the boys climbed out of the back and entered the camp. I was about to follow when a rough hand suddenly yanked me from the line. It was Lieutenant Sone. He brought me to his house, gave me a clean dry towel, and poured me a cup of tea.

We were sitting across from each other. He placed his hand on my neck and in faltering guttural sounds kept repeating the same sentence. Its passionate tone didn't elude me, but it puzzled me. I felt quite ill at ease, so I just smiled half-heartedly. After fifteen minutes he had a soldier give me a bunch of bananas so heavy I could hardly lift it. In addition he slipped me some cans of American corned beef. I looked for a place to sleep in the house on Trivelli Avenue where we had last lived before our transfer to Tangerang two months earlier. The women who were still there welcomed me warmly. They were extremely happy with the fruit and the cans of meat, too.

The next day I was transported to Cimahi by train together with several dozen other boys. The trip lasted twenty-four hours, although as the crow flies, it wasn't much more than a hundred kilometers. Since military transports were given priority, we were repeatedly parked on sidetracks for hours on end. We were crammed into open wooden third-class cars, so you could catch some wind while moving, which in the scorching heat of the day was very nice. Less pleasant were the sparks spraying from the locomotive that stung like fierce little bees. It caused a lot of hilarity. "Who in the world would travel third class? After all, isn't that only for the natives?" shouted one guy who always had something cheery to say. The guards, all of them heihos, had no replacements and were growing tired, too. When we weren't moving, local people often gave us fruit and water while the heihos turned a blind eye. They were glad to get a piece of the pie as well, for their fellow citizens were feeling sorry for them, too; and so they got their share.

In the middle of the night we came to a long standstill once again. Next to us another train, transporting troops, was sidetracked. The cars were jam-packed with weapons, backpacks, pieces of equipment, and soldiers. In the nocturnal silence you could hear the locomotives hiss in the distance and now and then the metal sound of cars being coupled. A man with a hammer attached to a long handle was checking the shafts by tapping on them, creating a spooky noise.

The trains stood side by side in complete silence. We were simply watching each other. The Japanese soldiers were just a few years older than we were—just boys. Filthy, sweaty, drained, and wan. Across the entire war theater from Manchuria to the Solomon Islands in the South Pacific, troops and soldiers were hauled hither and yon by the warlords in Tokyo.

"They've already been in that train for four days," the heihos told us. By early 1945 the mood throughout the land had grown extremely anti-Japanese. Consequently, those Japanese boys were not given any water or fruit by the people on the station platforms. The locals ignored them unequivocally. And we certainly wouldn't consider sharing anything with them either.

War is war.

Chapter 9

CIMAHI

Cimahi is a small mountain town just north of Bandung that for decades had been a large garrison town of the KNIL. Baros 6 was one of the regional internment camps where primarily boys were detained, although there was a limited number of adult men.

Dividing the camp in half, a busy thoroughfare was normally used by the town's inhabitants throughout the war. A number of sick old men were accommodated in the small section on the other side. The part where we lived was surrounded by a bamboo fence and had been a residential area of former non-commissioned officers.

With roughly twenty other boys I occupied a house on the edge of the camp. A covered gallery behind the house led to the bathroom, the kitchen, and a small room that was used as a pantry, the gudang, before the war. This is where the two men who ran our house slept, Mr. Boomslot and Hop, his assistant. I slept with eight boys in one room on beds made of wooden planks. At night we'd horse around across the beds and have pillow fights.

Mr. Boomslot always wore grubby khaki pants that had seen better times, as had their owner's body. His skin drooped over his belt because he had lost a lot of weight. He was a patient man with kind eyes that gazed through glasses held together by metal wire. He never raised his voice, never hit us, nor did he try to mother us. We soon noticed that he made no attempt to educate or instill any ideals in us either. Apparently, he had merely resolved to steer the group of boys safely through the war. That was a huge relief. I remember him with deep affection.

He established only a few house rules having to do with hygiene and order so that there would be some semblance of decency in the way we dealt with each other. He made sure we wouldn't get too dirty, that we'd sweep the rooms and shake out our sleeping mats every day. When you were sick, you knew he'd check on you from time to time. He made sure that the smallest boys weren't being bullied. More by his attitude than by doing anything concrete, he protected from our mockery a little Eurasian boy who was always crying and calling for his mother. There was a Jewish boy in our house who, stubbornly and on his own until the end of the war, kept the Sabbath by abstaining from all physical activities on Saturdays. Mr. Boomslot warned us to leave him in peace and not harass him. And that was just as well because young boys of twelve have very little compassion for, or understanding of, any divergent behavior.

His assistant Hop was much younger. He had pale eyes and short-cropped blond hair that still showed some waviness. He wanted to be addressed as "Hopman,"[7] but we called him "Hop," which irritated him. He told us not to, but there was very little he could do. It was our way of badgering him, and we fought a bitter battle with him over this until the very last day.

The first few weeks that we were under Hop's charge he tried to establish a regime based on the Boy Scouts, a regime from which we had just escaped in Tangerang. The other boys weren't very keen on it either. Supported by a neutrally dismissive position on the part of Mr. Boomslot, who apparently thought it was just nonsense, we managed to sabotage it quite effectively. We simply wouldn't do what he wanted. No matter what Hop did, we weren't participating.

One of the housemasters' important tasks was distributing the food that was brought in daily in large mess cans from the central kitchen. It was an important task because there wasn't much to distribute. In the rear gallery a place for each person was marked with a number where you had to put your plate or small pan.

---

7. *Hopman* means "scoutmaster" in Dutch.

Mr. Boomslot and Hop performed their chore with great care. We never doubted that everyone received exactly the same amount. Taking turns, you were allowed to lick the mess can clean after the food had been served. That was something we looked forward to for days in advance.

In the morning we had a portion of lumpy starch paste that had no flavor or nutritional value. Every once in a while you'd get a spoonful of brown sugar with it.

At noon they handed out a piece of gray, sticky bread that you'd try to get down with a mug of tea. And the evening meal consisted of wet rice or *ubi,* sweet potato, with a cooked vegetable, usually *kangkung,* a kind of leafy green, and sometimes a piece of tempeh or a quarter of an egg. We'd take tiny bites as slowly as we could and used a teaspoon as our utensil; it would take longer. By drinking a lot of water with it you began to feel full.

The last few months of the war we were really very hungry. We picked the wild purslane that grew everywhere on the side of the street and cooked soup with it on a wood fire. Once we caught a large frog and plopped him into the pot as well. But we didn't like the soup. Killing and cleaning the animal had been a lot of trouble, and we found it rather disgusting.

The camp leaders grew ubi, yams, in the small field in front of our house to supplement the scanty rations the Japanese gave us. During the night we'd sometimes furtively dig up the young tubers. They did taste good, but because we ate them raw we ended up with horrible stomach cramps later in the day, which not only were very painful but also proved that we'd been stealing.

The Japanese rules stated that in the camps we would be fed on the same basis as Japanese soldiers. It was a fine rule that could be flaunted at the International Red Cross, but I don't believe there was a single camp commander who ever followed it seriously.

Our commander, Lieutenant Kunimoto, occasionally tried to secure something extra for the boys, but his superiors didn't exactly appreciate it. One time he showed us the bruises he had sustained during one of those harsh refusals. Nevertheless, the smallest boys sporadically received some milk as a supplement. In exchange we provided him with quinine when he was on duty shaking with malaria. On Christmas 1944, we heard that he had made sure each internee would get three hundred grams of *nasi goreng,* fried rice, and on New Year's Eve he even provided *oliebollen.*

The camp was staffed by two officers, and the watch was made up of a few Japanese soldiers, a number of Koreans, and a platoon of heihos. We sometimes saw them drill with their wooden rifles. We were highly contemptuous of these poor guys. Yet we'd have conversations with them, we on one side of the fence and they on the other. They were extremely polite. They addressed us as sinyo, young man, and wanted to trade textiles for eggs or fruit. However, toward the end we didn't have much left to wear either. We spoke Malay with each other, and at times the conversations had a touch of intimacy. They told us that they had agreed to serve primarily to escape the poverty of their village.

It was almost as if we were partners in misfortune. They didn't know what was happening with the war, something we naturally were very curious about. "The Nippons don't know anything either," they'd say. "The Nippons are desperate." They also told us about the lack of food, the lack of textiles, and the many diseases from which the native population suffered during the last year of the war.

Increasingly, the food shortages also made us ill, ill with the same diseases that the native population had suffered since time immemorial.

There was beri-beri, which made your legs swell up and was caused by vitamin deficiency. Eurasian boys, some of whom were living in the camp, taught us a simple remedy for this condition. *Cabe rawit* grew wild on small bushes everywhere along the road; these were little bright red chili peppers, no bigger than two centimeters. They are so hot that they cause instant blisters when you rub them on your skin. But they're loaded with vitamins. When you are vitamin-deficient, you eat them without any problem, like candy; then when your tongue starts burning again, you know your vitamin deficiency has been cured. As soon as two weeks after the Japanese capitulation you wouldn't think of putting one in your mouth again: you knew right away that your deficiency was cured.

Everyone suffered from dysentery. The bloody, watery diarrhea would squirt from your body as often as twenty times a day, making you weak and dizzy. When you felt the urge again, you'd run to the squat-latrine. Soaking in sweat and trembling, you'd sit above the hole while the liquid poured from your body. We called it "racing shit" because you had to be fast. Otherwise, if you didn't make it in time, you had to wash your own pair of pants, and then, while the other boys laughed and jeered, you'd sit naked as you waited for the sun to dry them.

Small wounds or cuts easily became infected. The red line of blood poisoning would crawl below the skin along your thigh up to your groin. Before you knew it, you had a wound on your foot that was as large as a silver dollar and wouldn't heal. They were known as "coolie sores." After the war they healed rapidly, at least ours did. I fear that for the coolies it took a lot longer.

The heihos were terrified of their Japanese superiors. Whenever an officer approached, they'd quickly take to their heels like chickens fleeing from a fox, to our great glee. When they overstepped the line, they were brutally flogged right in front of the gate. They had to lower their pants and were whipped with a leather belt. Then they had to stand at attention in the sun for hours. At that point we really did feel sorry for them. One time one of them was caught trading the watch of an internee for a few eggs and a bunch of bananas. They suspended him for twenty-four hours from a wooden structure with barbed wire, known as a martingale, his back raw and bleeding. We felt enormous pity for him.

The Korean soldiers were stocky, rustic types with round faces, who paid little attention to us.

In the morning there was roll call. We'd be shivering in the chilly early morning mountain wind.

To protect us from head lice they had shaven our heads, an effective remedy. We had no body lice, but we did have bedbugs, round, reddish-brown insects that bit us and caused itching lumps on our skin. They stuck together in tight little groups in the cracks in the wall and between the boards of our beds. When you squashed them, the blood sprayed everywhere and emitted a strong odor of decayed almonds. We made drawings on the wall by waiting for a louse to crawl by and then, just at the right moment, crush it and draw the line of blood right where you wanted it.

The Japanese were renowned for their exaggerated concern, not to say hysteria, with hygiene, especially for themselves. Our bedbug plague became too much for them. One day the Japanese authorities decided that each individual had to hand in twenty dead bedbugs a day during morning roll call. Usually they were carefully counted. This battle worked so efficiently that it soon brought us into difficulty: it became harder and harder to gather the required number of bedbugs. You risked a whack on the head if you were short. Fortunately, there was a house on the other side with sick, elderly men that was overrun with bedbugs, and so the supply was guaranteed. However, the house was extremely squalid and stank horribly, so then we decided to cultivate the bugs ourselves. A lively trade in dead bugs was the result. We also used them among ourselves as payment, to buy off a chore for example.

Roll call was usually taken by a Korean corporal who would quickly ride by on one of the few wobbly-looking bikes that before the war you could buy everywhere for *fl.* 2.50. These roll calls were different from what we were used to in the women's camp where they were very boring, as they lasted forever, or because the count was off, or the smaller children were crying, or the women didn't bow properly. However, in Cimahi it went relatively fast. It seemed that the Koreans weren't very keen on this chore either. We knew it would go especially fast when the fat corporal, whom we called "Dirk," approached, and we'd make only a half-hearted attempt at any discipline or other form of correct conduct.

One morning the commander himself came to take roll call. Lieutenant Kunimoto, a twenty-two-year-old Japanese Korean, was a nice enough guy. But he was in a bad mood that day. He and his colleagues had already spent more than three years on Java, and Japan didn't give any periodical furloughs. Perhaps he had heard of the heartless fire bombings by which the Americans had turned entire Japanese cities to ashes in one night; perhaps he was worried about his parents or his sweetheart somewhere in Japan. We didn't know the reason at the time, and, even if we had known, it would have left us completely cold. Our rules were simple but very clear, such as "Your own fault," or "He that mischief hatches, mischief catches," and for the rest we didn't pay it any mind.

Lieutenant Kunimoto took roll call seriously. It so happened that the boy in front of me didn't have enough dead bedbugs to hand in. Kunimoto pressured him, and I allowed myself a little joke, saying something like "That officer thinks you're nothing but a dope, Kees."

Before I knew it I'd received a solid boxing around the ears. I was seeing stars. It had been a very long time since I'd been hit like that; before the war my father would occasionally give me a slap in the face. After that morning I stayed out of Kunimoto's way as much as I could.

During the day we usually just messed around. We didn't have any marbles, balls, or roller skates in the boys' camp, of course. But we didn't miss them. We had no need for rowdy games, as our energy level had dwindled. We played Monopoly or Sorry, or we just lazed around.

In a previous phase this had been a women's camp. A small youth library had been abandoned in the house next door that apparently had escaped the scrutiny of the Japanese. I discovered the joy of reading and must have read the *Courier of the Czar,* bound in blue, at least three times. I devoured a whole set of Karl May.[8] To my annoyance, Old Shatterhand and Winnetou with his silver rifle just couldn't manage to catch Santer, the murderer of Winnetou's father. I spent entire afternoons reading.

---

8. Karl May (1842–1912) was a German writer famous for his adventure novels set in the American Old West.

The men in the camp attempted to arrange some education for us. It made them look good, but we had long ago become unaccustomed to regular schooling and found it pretty disagreeable. They taught us in small groups, subjects such as language, basic math, and geography, either in the morning or the afternoon. We played hooky as often as we could, arrived late, and made a racket during the lessons. It didn't bother us in the least that much of the teaching fell apart and happened irregularly because it had to be done in secret. It didn't go on for very long; the men no longer had the strength to keep us on our toes.

Sometimes we had chores to do: sweep the street, clear the drains, jobs like that. The Dutch camp leadership occasionally arranged for us to do chores outside the camp. Higher up in the mountains there was an experimental farm from the earlier Dutch colonial period, known as Leuwigajah, a large enterprise with extensive fields and pastures. There were cows in the pasture and pigs inside their pens. We had to weed the vegetable beds, clean the pens, and take care of the animals. In the afternoon they would slaughter a few pigs for the Japanese garrison in Cimahi.

We were eager for this chore. You were outside the camp—an outing in itself—and in the fresh air. They gave you extra food, and you didn't really have to work too hard. We slacked off considerably. If ever there was a Japanese soldier checking up on us we would alert each other, and we quickly learned to display the ignorant behavior of the subservient. "Just act like a stupid coolie," we told each other, "and nothing will happen to you." You even got paid, fourteen cents a day, whereupon in the afternoon on the way back we'd do some excellent business with the heihos who'd buy food or fruit along the roadside for us. Furthermore, we smuggled the intestines of the slaughtered pigs into the camp, which were welcome in the central kitchen and actually added a few thin rings of fat around the soup pot.

One afternoon—I now know that it must have been in June 1945—a Korean soldier came to get me and brought me to the Japanese commander's house, a villa right near the gate. There

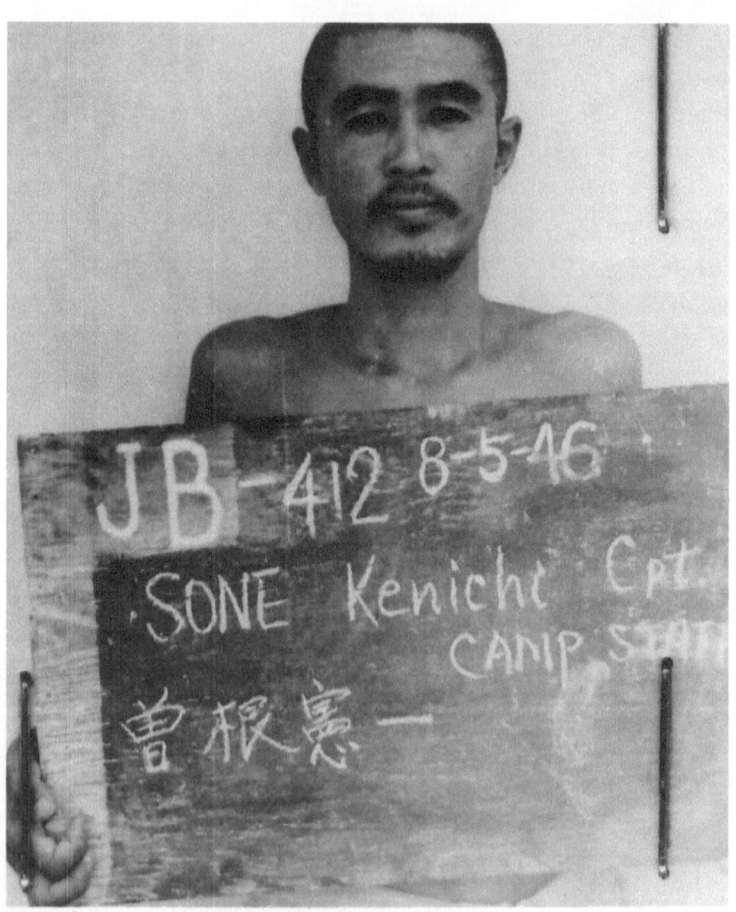

Identification photo of Captain Sone after his arrest.

was Sone, who apparently had come to visit me. He looked me over carefully while talking to Kunimoto, who responded with brief sounds: "Hai, hai, hai." I was just sitting there, feeling uncomfortable, yet at the same time I caught myself quite appreciating his visit and can't deny that I felt a certain fondness for this Japanese officer.

Again he gave me fruit and other edibles to take along, which my housemates thoroughly enjoyed.

It was the last time I would see Sone Kenichi. Although we didn't know it yet, the war was coming to an end. One afternoon in late August 1945 a plane suddenly flew over with a red-white-and-blue circle on its wings. It was flying so low that we could see the white faces of the cheerfully waving airmen. For days rumors had already been going through the camp about a huge bomb that had been dropped on two Japanese cities. They were more than rumors. We knew, or at least strongly suspected, that some of the men in the camp were listening to Australian radio broadcasts with secret small crystal receiver sets. Of course that was strictly forbidden by the Japanese, and we were worried that our Mr. Boomslot and Hop had hidden a similar set in the house, too, in the nook of their little room next to the bathroom. If discovered, the entire house would be collectively punished, and you would have to stand facing each other and hit the boy across from you in the face. If you didn't smack him hard enough the Korean soldiers would show you how it was supposed to be done. And that *really* hurt. Besides, hitting gently brings no comfort in the long run: if you keep it up long enough it will begin to hurt all by itself. It had already happened to us once, and we had absolutely no desire to see it happen again.

But Mr. Boomslot and Hop didn't flinch. "Don't you worry," is all they said.

More than fifty years later, in 2003, I visited the two afflicted Japanese cities, Hiroshima and Nagasaki. Hiroshima's icon, the round dome of the burnt-out office, affected me profoundly. It was an early bright spring morning. I stood near the bridge that had been the target of the pilot of the *Enola Gay*. I looked at the dome, and it was as if a burden fell off my shoulders—I can't express it any other way. I was liberated from an oppression for which I have no further name. Strangely enough, I wasn't thinking of the victims of the bombings themselves or of all the other dead of the Pacific War, but of the Japanese soldiers and officers who had played a role in my youth.

The rest of the environment, the "Peace Park," and the large exhibit farther along enthralled me less. They really barrage you with "Peace" while the Pacific War is mentioned with far too much detachment. When I read the caption of a photo that stated that "in 1937 the China incident happened," it became too much for me, and I left in disgust. In reality the so-called "China incident" was a large-scale war of aggression that didn't just "happen" but had been set up and executed as a conscious and brutal campaign of conquest in North China.

The visit to Nagasaki, however, was incredibly impressive. The city is located on a magnificent bay with beautiful nineteenth-century colonial-style villas in the hills. The memorial center is simple, modest, thoughtful, and doesn't avoid the painful issues. Thus, there are extensive reports on the experience of the city's Koreans who, as second-class citizens, suffered disproportionately from the atomic attack.

Every year on the 6th and 9th of August the fate of these two cities still haunts me. At the time we were gloating; now I don't know what to think anymore. What is certain is that the atom bomb spared human lives, for in the camps and in the occupied areas outside of them, too, the situation had grown dire, and complete attrition was common. When taking cognizance of the bloody price that was paid for conquering a little island like Iwo Jima, you can't begin to imagine the price that an invasion of Japan's main island would have involved: thousands, if not tens of thousands of American marines killed in the first few days alone. Not to mention the fate of the Japanese civilian population. Unscrupulous, the governing clique in Tokyo was prepared to sacrifice the country and the people in their entirety, as had happened with the American conquest of the island of Okinawa, for example. But it remains an infernal weapon, nevertheless.

During that same visit to Japan I bought a replica of the headband that the Japanese kamikaze fliers wore in 1945, which showed a red circle and a few Japanese characters. "What does this text say?" I asked the salesman. "It means: victory is certain, victory is ours, Sir," he replied. "Really fine, isn't it?" I exclaimed. "Please let me have that headband," and I paid him. I found it hard to repress a grim satisfaction.

For us the war suddenly came to an end in August 1945. Just like that, without any ceremony or fuss. The camp commander summoned the Dutch camp leaders to come and see him and, without entering into any details, announced that the war was over. No bombings, no artillery fires, no street battles. It felt a bit anticlimactic to me.

Peace was here.

The Korean soldiers who guarded us were unmoved. But that night we heard a commotion in their quarters, and there was shooting going on. "The Koreans are rising in mutiny," one man said.

The watch was taken over by Japanese soldiers whom their officers apparently trusted more. A few days after the capitulation Admiral Mountbatten, the commander-in-chief of the Allied troops, had ordered that for their own safety the internees were to remain in the camps. But the admiral was of no concern to us, and we crawled out underneath the fence to physically enjoy our newly found freedom. You were able to purchase food—fruit and eggs—at the small market that had emerged at the gate. The few clothes that some of us still had found eager buyers, which was understandable as the population was going around in rags.

The market women and the older men were courteous and nice, but the young Indonesians were far from friendly. Many little red-and-white flags were flying from the *warungs,* the vending stalls, and the little village houses. Right they are, it's their country, I thought, and I still believe that. In my naïveté I said so out loud, which didn't do me any good. One man called it "high treason," but that didn't change my mind.

Food attached to parachutes was falling from the sky in those days. Right after the war that actually turned out to be quite perilous for a while because the Allied pilots truly enjoyed their assignment and in their enthusiasm weren't always careful. One time a cylinder with canned cheese, corned beef, and chocolate crashed right through the roof of a neighboring house. The stuff was stuck way up in the rafters, really making us laugh. Not every parachute would open, and then the crates and metal containers would slam left and right into the ground and explode. Clumps of soil, dried apricots, cartons of cigarettes, cans of pineapple, and condoms were flying around your head.

I wanted to leave, something the Allied authorities didn't permit; under those chaotic circumstances it was a wise move, although nobody paid any attention to it. Many of the men and boys departed, an act known as *bolos,* truancy.

One of my mother's brothers was in a large men's camp in Bandung. He sent me a message inviting me to join him, so I decided to leave. It wasn't very far, and in September 1945 trams and trains were still traveling safely between Cimahi and Bandung.

Mr. Boomslot shook my hand. "Home you go, my boy," he said.

Chapter 10

BANDUNG

In early October 1945 I spent a few weeks with my uncle in a large men's camp in the heart of the city of Bandung. It was being guarded by Gurkhas, professional Nepalese soldiers of the British colonial army. The Allied authorities had sent them to Java to protect the internment camps. It was the time when the *bersiap*, the bloody phase of the revolution, began, and Bandung was in a state of unrest. Every so often my uncle and I would go downtown to shop but also to experience freedom. It was once again possible, but not without risk. You could see young Indonesian freedom fighters walking around the side streets and alleyways with clenched fists, shouting revolutionary slogans. Some of them wore their hair long, having sworn not to cut it until Indonesia was liberated. They had also sworn an oath of celibacy for the duration, and this could not have been easy since it would be four more years to independence. And no one ever mentions the reaction of their girlfriends. These young men were armed with sharply pointed bamboo spears, a lethal weapon. Gurkhas patrolled the main shopping streets.

My uncle, too, was eager to do something about my education. He tried to give me language and math lessons. But I much preferred the company of the Gurkhas and hung out with them all day long.

They were friendly and detached; they smelled of pepper and other spices. They had long Lee-Enfield rifles from World War I, with bolts that opened and closed and a large round knob to push the copper bullets into the chamber. The Gurkhas were feared warriors, as they still are today, always deployed when the British Empire—or what's left of it—wishes to use military force. In 1982

I read in the newspaper that they were going to be deployed in the war in the Falkland Islands. Remembering their curved daggers, I pitied the Argentine soldiers in advance.

They had placed sandbags as fortifications around the camp.

Bren guns on bipods stood between them every five meters or so. The soldiers gave me cigarettes that I smoked as if I'd never done anything else in my life, and they'd send me outside the perimeter to buy food for them at one of the nearby stalls.

They taught me to sing *God shave the King*, and, albeit a little odd, I believed for years that this was the right text of the English national anthem.

They let me help them clean their weapons and fill the metal magazines of the Bren guns. I would hand them the bullets, and they'd carefully push them in. The weapons smelled of refined oil. When I entered military service some ten years later, I suddenly recognized the smell of that oil, and for a moment I was back in Bandung on the lawn with the Gurkhas.

Late one evening—I was already lying on my *tikar,* my sleeping mat—there was the sound of gunshots and the Brens' dull rattle outside. The Gurkhas were beating off an attack on the camp by the pemudas. "They're slaughtering the extremists," a man who lay beside me said, "you can leave them to it."

The next morning I rushed off to my Ghurka friends, who greeted me effusively as always. One of them looked at me, pointed at the Bren, and said "Pow, pow, pow," tapped his chest, made a horizontal gesture across his throat with the back of his hand, uttered a long-drawn-out "ggggrrrttt," laughed uproariously and playfully pulled my ear.

My parents were most likely in Batavia, now called Jakarta, and although that wasn't certain at all, my uncle decided I should try to join them. The trains from Bandung to Batavia were still running but were more and more frequently assaulted by freedom fighters and gangs of robbers, episodes during which all white people were killed. This is why my uncle found me a seat on a British military plane that maintained the connection between the two cities.

The Gurkhas brought me to the Andir Airport in an open army truck preceded by a rattling half-track. The ride was interrupted several times. Something was wrong. In the silence of the afternoon I could hear the quiet clicking of the safety catches being pulled. The Gurkhas were nervous. I must have had at least six guards around me, each holding his rifle horizontally with his finger on the trigger. I wasn't scared, just hoping to turn around and go back because I really didn't want to leave Bandung.

A British pilot in a leather jacket with a sheepskin collar hoisted me up into his plane and quite forcefully dragged me by my neck to the front. Seated in the glass machine gun turret in the nose of the Catalina, I flew to Jakarta. It was terribly drafty in the canopy, and I was freezing in the worn-out shirt I had put on for the occasion.

Chapter 11

JAKARTA

I had been told that my parents were probably in Jakarta, but I didn't know where. When the English plane landed at Kemayoran Airport, I had not seen my father in three and a half years. He had fled to Bandung with the governor-general and his staff in early 1942. I had said good-bye to my mother in Tangerang ten months earlier when they transferred me to the boys' camp.

I got a ride in an English jeep to the large women's camp of Cideng, the only place in Jakarta I was familiar with. Cideng looked desolate, completely different from the year before when I'd left with my mother and sister. It was a terrible sight. Everything was filthy, dirty, with broken household goods strewn everywhere, the gardens now neglected quagmires with foul-smelling, greenish pools of water, the houses in ruins. Everything wooden had been burned. The yards were trampled and strewn with primitive fireplaces and wrecked pots and rusty tins. Every cesspool was overflowing, and the drainage pipes were clogged with fetid brown ooze. It smelled of shit and lice, and flies were swarming everywhere. The place was crawling with thousands of hollow-eyed women and emaciated children. It was no wonder that when she visited Cideng in October 1945 during an inspection tour of the camps Lady Mountbatten burst into tears.

In the camp's office they took down my name and promised they would check on my parents' whereabouts. "Do you have a place to sleep?" they asked. I told them I did, even though it wasn't true, and walked out the gate. I hooked up with a boy who found himself in the same situation, and we went to a large, low, cool, abandoned colonial house located outside the camp in a district just a few minutes' walk away. We moved in without asking permission from anyone. Besides, we wouldn't have known whom to ask and didn't worry about it for a second. Some other boys had already settled in before us, and we really used the house only to sleep and take showers.

At that time Jakarta was a seething mayhem. Allied troops had landed only in late September 1945, and there were far too few of them. Revolutionary pemudas unleashed a savage urban insurrection. Houses went up in flames. The smell of smoke and echoes of gunfire were everywhere, and one could be shot at any moment from moving trams that were painted with anti-Dutch slogans. There was much looting, and bodies were floating in the Molenvliet Canal. Brown bodies usually, because in this revolution, too, many ethnic conflicts were being settled.

Actually, the only safe place was inside the camp, which for a time was still guarded by the Japanese. I thought that was pretty funny, especially when they'd greet you with a slight bow instead of the reverse, as had been the case throughout the war.

There was no more hunger. Stalls and food stands were set up near the gates on the other side of the bridge across the Cideng Canal after the Japanese capitulated. In the morning I'd go there and have a few *lempers* for breakfast, sticky rice cooked in coconut milk with bits of spiced meat rolled in a banana leaf. I loved them and am still very fond of them today. Unfortunately, in Amsterdam they are now prepared in wraps of plastic instead of banana leaf so that a touch of the green aroma is missing.

Those were good days. Nobody paid any attention to me; nobody asked or expected anything from me. I was left entirely to my own devices and thoroughly enjoyed it. It was thrilling and exciting. I have no idea whether it was foolhardiness or whether I am naturally reckless, but I was never afraid, not even for a second, despite the shooting, the burning, the shouting in the distance, and the constant threats around me. I was living life as if in a boys' adventure book.

I have never again been as free as I was those ten days.

During the day we hung around the camp gate. A Red Cross station had been installed in a large villa, mainly concerned with collecting and distributing data to inform people of the whereabouts and fate of their relatives. I earned money as a messenger boy. Many telegrams and letters needed to be delivered inside the camp where I, of course, knew how to get around quite well. Initially, I sought out the women in their overcrowded houses and gave them the messages, which often caused great joy and emotion. It was frequently the first sign of life in years from a husband, son, or lover.

Then, after a few days, something unexpected happened. One woman didn't dare open the message and asked me to read it to her. It consisted of a few lines in official language. I didn't understand the text literally but gathered its meaning. It was a death notice. I stood there, frozen and speechless, not knowing what to do or say. In my panic I stuffed the piece of paper in her hand and took to my heels. From then on I never opened another message when I was asked to.

And then I found my parents again, or, rather, my father found me.

One day, having just delivered a telegram to someone in the camp, I returned to the gate. On the bridge of Trivelli Avenue a tall, slender man approached me. He was dressed in a brand-new, starched American khaki uniform, a short-sleeved shirt, and sharply creased pants. He was carrying a gun attached to his belt. I recognized him instantly, more by his bearing than his face.

We embraced each other. "Freddy, my boy," he said.

I put my head on his shoulder. His shirt was freshly ironed and smelled deliciously of starch and soap and of the cigarettes from a small round can, Player's Navy Cut, which he smoked nonstop.

I was happy but at the same time was unable to repress a sense of regret. I had my father back, but I had lost my freedom.

Chapter 12

ADEK

Adek was the abbreviation for Algemeen Delisch Emigratie Kantoor (General Deli Emigration Office). It was a complex of buildings in the southern part of Jakarta, an area known as Meester Cornelis. The Dutch government had built it during the colonial period as a temporary accommodation for migrating laborers. Despite its fancy title, I suspect that it was no more than a shelter for recently hired Deli contract workers and other poor wretches.

The Japanese had used it as an internment camp for women. My father knew that my mother and sister were there. He brought me to them, and that is how I was reunited with the members of my family, to put it somewhat formally. Of course, I was happy to see my mother and Carolien again, but the strange thing is that I have no recollection of that reunion at all. It amazes me as I write this down, but that's just the way it is. I can't explain it. Had the past two months left me with too many impressions and experiences? Did I repress it because it meant that my little life of freedom had come to a definite end? I don't know, and there's not much point in speculating.

My father was still bivouacked in the barracks of the so-called Tenth Battalion, where he had spent the entire war as a POW. He stayed after the Japanese capitulation because he had work and responsibilities there. I remained in Adek with my mother, expecting to join my father within a few days.

I was too old to sleep in the women's barracks and was therefore placed in another part of Adek, since it was for only a short time.

I slept with a platoon of Sikhs who were proud soldiers of the British Empire, charged with the security and surveillance of this women's camp. A good thing, too, for it was close to a city kampung that was overrun with pugnacious, raucous pemudas. As is all too common in restless times, there was a lot of robbery and looting in the neighborhood.

The Sikhs were slender, with dark eyes and long black hair, which for religious reasons they were not allowed to cut and wore wrapped in a piece of fabric like a turban.

They gave me a cot in their dormitory. At the end of the day after their duties were done, they attended to their equipment, their weapons, themselves, and each other in a state of near nudity. After showering they'd sit across from or behind one another, drying their long hair at great length with a cloth, laying it out in tresses, which they carefully wrapped around the head. They'd also depilate or massage each other's shoulders, while conversing quietly in a softly babbling stream of sounds. Of course, I didn't understand them.

Their washroom was used by me as well. It was a tiled space with a row of showers. One afternoon I was taking a shower in the presence of a few Sikhs. The man standing next to me suddenly placed his hand carefully between my legs and gently kneaded me with an up and down motion. His face was directed upward, and in a toneless voice he spoke some words. It did startle me, but it never occurred to me to resist. He wasn't hurting me, and it didn't last very long. I never told anyone about the incident, not even my parents. As far as I know, it didn't leave me with any complexes or trauma. It simply happened, and that was all.

Chapter 13

THE 10TH BATTALION

Inside the power vacuum that was created in Batavia after the Japanese capitulation from mid-August 1945 on, the government almost automatically fell to the military, to which authority was now ascribed in spite of itself. During those first chaotic weeks, my father, together with the British liaison officer and secret agent Lieutenant Colonel Laurens van der Post attempted to maintain a minimum of law and order. Van der Post had parachuted into the interior of western Java in June 1942 to organize the resistance against the Japanese invaders. A naïve idea. With his striking, tall carriage and his white head amid the indigenous population, he was taken captive almost instantly, of course, and spent the rest of the war chafing at the bit in the 10th Battalion, the POW camp in the center of Jakarta where my father was the leader of the imprisoned men.

It was a task that had truly exhausted my father, understandably so when you realize what an irregular bunch of prisoners inhabited the camp: coarse Australian hooligans, unruly European KNIL fusiliers, and desperate Moluccan KNIL troops. In 1942 the latter refused to take a loyalty oath to the new Japanese rulers and therefore had not been let go as most of the other native soldiers were. It was highly virtuous of them, but it didn't make them any less troublesome in the everyday interaction of their imprisonment.

In 1985 Laurens van der Post wrote me: "You have every reason to be proud of your father. He was one of the outstanding officers, a distinguished person." It is the sole sign of appreciation of my father that I am aware of.

My father's responsibilities were increased even more because, during the first weeks after the Japanese capitulation, the 10th

Battalion had become the refuge for all those who feared revolutionary violence: Chinese, Dutch Eurasians, and Moluccan families.

A few days after I arrived in Adek my father came to pick us up. We occupied a house across from the barracks gate, which was safe, as it was situated close to the guards. A number of Moluccan military families were housed there as well.

The men were covered in pistols, Sten guns, and carbines. They held intense grudges against the nationalists and the revolutionary youth who were extremely active in the city. Like almost all the KNIL officers, my father had a soft spot for the Moluccans. "But," he commented, "these days they are a little trigger-happy."

During the day I played with a Moluccan boy my age. We weren't allowed to leave the yard. In the old central section of the city there was heavy looting going on, and the Chinese were the victims of popular fury and pogroms. A few uprooted Chinese families lived next door to us hoping to find protection in the proximity of the army barracks. I watched the Cinas, as the Eurasian boys called them, felt sorry for them, and regretted ever having thrown stones at their shops.

The sounds of shouting and explosions could be heard in the distance.

My friend and I would sit on a low brick wall that separated the garden from the street. There was always a lot to look at. Men in jeeps or private cars came and went. Sharp whistling noises could be heard several times a day, and a moment later soldiers would come outside at a jog, taking up positions behind trees and low walls. And they'd send us indoors.

"*Lekas, lekas,* quick, quick," they called, and "*Awas,* be careful." Snipers had been sighted in the area.

Usually we could just watch the trucks being unloaded, the officers coming and going, the movements of the guards, and the departure of army trucks full of soldiers.

Sometimes a jeep passed by with a large, highly visible British flag attached to the antenna, which is how they made it clear they had no desire to become involved in the colonial conflict of the Dutch. "Tssk," my friend hissed through his teeth contemptuously, "the *Inggris* won't fight." The British were not keen on stirring up the Indonesian hornets' nest. Under the aegis of "that half-naked fakir," as Churchill referred to Gandhi, the nationalist movement in India was quite strong. The British didn't know how much they could actually trust their Indian troops. In any case, the latter demonstrated little interest in armed confrontations with the Indonesian combat groups, and certainly not in dying that way. And one could hardly blame them.

My friend wanted to know if I'd been hungry in the camp and what my favorite food was. I told him and asked: "What about you?" "Rice with dog," he replied.

One day there was loud wailing in the back of the house. One of their young men had been shot from a car and killed. That night my mother hid me and my sister under the bed. "Just to be safe; it won't last long," she said. "Something's about to happen and I don't know what."

Shortly thereafter we heard angry footsteps on the gravel in the garden and many heated voices. Fierce shooting followed, very close to the back of the house. Revenge: the kampung just a little further on was burning like a torch. The next morning the gray flakes of ash were still fluttering down.

I heard but never saw the "extremists," as they called the fanatic youth that waged the battle for their republic. Not alive at least.

A truck passed our house late one afternoon at the end of a long day of shooting in a nearby neighborhood. I was drinking tea with my parents on the terrace in the front yard. All of a sudden I saw that the truck was loaded with a pile of dead native youths, their clothes dirty, ripped, and stained with blood. Revulsion shook me.

The guard at the gate spat in their direction. Standing in the street, my Moluccan friend did the same.

I will never forget this image as long as I live.

Chapter 14

TANJUNG PRIOK

A few days later, at the end of November 1945, we were in Tanjung Priok, Jakarta's harbor, where we embarked on a small, bare, squalid trading ship. It wasn't much bigger than a coaster and was supposed to take us to Singapore where the large troop ship the *New Amsterdam* was waiting to take repatriates to Holland.

The small coaster had a crew of British Indian sailors. Since there were only a few cabins, the passengers, several dozen European men, women, and children, stayed on deck and in the hallways.

Sometime in the midafternoon the small vessel was unmoored from the wharf. We were departing. In the hazy distance I saw the mountains and volcanoes of Java and knew I wouldn't see them again any time soon. Once we were on the high seas, I stood at the rusty railing, looking at the foam on the waves and at the seabirds flying along above the thruster wake of the ship in the Java Sea. They dived fearlessly into the churning water preying on fish floating upward.

Evening had fallen, and it was time to find a place to sleep. My mother and sister had been assigned to one of the few passenger cabins. My father was attending a meeting with the ship's officers. "Go find yourself a spot somewhere," he said, "it's only for one night." I found a niche at the end of a dark hallway where it smelled of oil, with cockroaches rustling everywhere; that's where I made myself a bed of cloths and rags and went to sleep.

In the middle of the night someone was yanking my shoulder. I looked into the dark, sweaty face of a sailor. He wasn't particularly friendly and said something. I couldn't understand him but with a gesture of his hand and thumb he made his wish known. The message was clear: "Buzz off, this is my spot."

I was being thrown out of Asia.

Chapter 15

RITE OF PASSAGE

When we sailed into the port of Singapore the next morning, it turned out that the *New Amsterdam* had left a few hours before. The city's British administration improvised a shelter for the homeless group from Java. They put us up in a company building of the large barracks of the British army, just outside the city. Soldiers of the occupying Japanese army had been bivouacked there until only a short time before, but they were locked up as POWs elsewhere and were far less comfortable now. The buildings and grounds were in excellent condition and well maintained.

We slept in the spacious halls of the company building on simple wooden beds with mosquito nets. Men, women, and children together. "It's just for a few weeks, after all," the British commander said. The food was prepared in a bleak canteen in the garrison's kitchen. The oatmeal they served for breakfast was so thick that your spoon would stand up in it vertically. It tasted really good, a horse of a different color from the watery starch paste in the boys' camp. The rest of the food, too, was decent and nutritious. "Army food, army shit!" the dark-skinned mess hall soldiers who served us said apologetically, but I ate this "shit" with relish.

One week went by, two weeks went by. December went by, it was the new year of 1946, and my thirteenth birthday went by unnoticed. Because we might have to leave any moment, our stay continued to be makeshift. Nothing long-term was organized, no distractions, no entertainment. We children hung around all day long in the empty drill field. There wasn't even an old tennis ball to play an exciting game of stickball with.

Early in February 1946, after a two-month waiting period, we finally embarked on a jam-packed repatriate ship, the *Alcantara,* an British passenger ship that had been turned into a troop ship during the war.

They assigned me a place to sleep in the corner of one of the holds. It smelled of tar, oil, brackish water, and unwashed clothes. The long wooden tables and benches were screwed into the floor. The rest was all metal: the floor, the steep stairs to the deck and to the holds below, the bulkheads, the joists with their hexagon rivets. Large round lamps, protected by grates, burned all day long and provided a feeble glow at night.

The many men and boys slept in hammocks suspended from hooks especially attached for this purpose. They swung languidly back and forth with the undulation of the large gray ship. I found the hammock uncomfortable, and all through the journey I just couldn't get used to it. Often I couldn't fall asleep, and in the silence of the night I'd listen to the rhythmical creaking of the ropes, to the sounds and the mumbling of those who slept, and to the bumping around of people going to the toilet in the half-light, up and down the steep stairs in their wooden sandals.

On the other side of the ship's walls you could hear the swirling and churning of the seawater. Sometimes a hard object would make a loud bang against the ship, a tree trunk floating on the sea. Once in a great while you could feel a change in the vibration of the *Alcantara,* and you realized it was moving more slowly. The seas were still full of mines. In the daytime there was always a sailor high up in a kind of cage in the foremost mast, on the outlook for drifting sea mines. In the cramped confines of the hold I found this a pretty scary notion. If we hit a mine, I thought, the water will come rushing in here, and I'll drown.

Right next to me were two men, brothers or friends, who were very close with each other. I was able to hear their whispered conversation; always one spoke while the other listened and in a soft encouraging voice gave frequent brief answers: "Yes, Jan, of course."

The first one talked and talked: "I said to her let's just try again.... I said what's wrong with you, every day for three and a half years I've been thinking of you and longing for you.... I want it to be the way it was, the way it was before, before the war."

I listened without wanting to. What I heard worried me vaguely, and I repressed thoughts about my parents.

In the morning there was a long loud bell, and then the lights came on full strength. No one was paying any particular attention to me. I got up, rolled up my hammock in the musty air just like the others, and hung it on a metal hook. You showered with seawater that stung every little wound and cut you had and made you feel sticky all day long.

After breakfast I wandered around the decks. When the ship pitched and quaked in a storm and it smelled like vomit everywhere inside, it was wonderfully quiet on deck. I loved it. In those four weeks on board the ship I liked being alone and had no need for any contact with other people.

Generally, the weather was calm and the decks were then filled with people walking and talking. The adults talked only about where they had been interned and what it had been like.

The lanky boys and girls were often together in large groups, laughing and horsing around. Frequently, one of the boys had a guitar or an accordion. They'd sing "Don't Fence Me In" and other American songs, but I never felt like joining them.

They had organized academic classes in the afternoon. I learned spelling, did writing exercises, and had to do math with decimals and long division.

The geography lessons were taught by a little old Eurasian man. During one topographical exercise it was my turn and I had to name the islands of the Indies archipelago, at which he pointed on a teaching map. I couldn't get beyond the four large islands (Java, Sumatra, Borneo, and Sulawesi).

"What?" the little man yelled in a heavy Indies accent. "Don't you even know your motherland?"

Of course I do, I thought to myself. Of course I know that land, the scent of the soil, the taste of the sweet *pisang susu,* the little milk banana, the cooing of the *perkutut,* the turtledove, the wonderful feeling of leaning against Hatih the laundress's hip and listening to her words as she was folding the clothes to be ironed. I despised that little man with his stupid tiny islands.

Later that day I overheard a mother tell her child: "In a few weeks we'll be in Coevorden. The Dutch climate will do you good. It is the heart of winter right now."

"Holland is your fatherland," my father had told me not long before; it had sounded rather solemn.

Winter, Holland, fatherland, motherland: it all meant very little to me, and I really didn't want to think about it either.

When at all possible I'd go to the bow of the ship and sit down on a stack of cables. I'd lean against the thickly painted railing and look at the waves of the green sea, the clouds, and the flying fish jumping up high from the backwash and floating away above the water in a wide arc. Sometimes dolphins would swim along for hours on end, tumbling and toppling, able to change speed very quickly. A British sailor passing by said something. I couldn't understand it, but his tone was friendly, just as all the crew members were. I'd sit there for hours. No one bothered me, and so I could appease my thoughts a bit. I had not missed my parents when they weren't there; now that they were present I missed them.

Every evening I went to the small movie auditorium at the back of the ship. I always made sure to be on time because it was very popular. They showed two films: *The Woman in the Window* in black-and-white, and *Bathing Beauty,* which was in color and had many water ballets. At night the images of the long slender legs of the women and their breasts, hips, and buttocks in the tightly fitting, shiny bathing suits wouldn't let go of me. I didn't know if I was supposed to be ashamed of that, but I couldn't share it with anyone.

I didn't see my mother very often. She was somewhere in the middle of the ship in one of the cabins, where they had hallways with stairs and carpets. That part of the ship had not been altered and exuded a prewar luxury. Actually, I hardly ever went there.

Sometimes I'd run into Carolien on one of the decks. She was usually with a few girlfriends, giggling and pushing each other up against one of the big boys or one of the British sailors. Stupid chicks.

"Where do you hang out all day long?" she asked me once. "Mamma would like you to stop by some time."

The RAPWI—Recovery of Allied Prisoners of War and Internees—which organized the repatriation of Europeans from Asia, had asked my father to assume leadership of the Dutch passengers. Many of the people were ill; there were arguments and problems of food and hygiene on board with the several thousand individuals who were in poor condition and at the end of their rope, mentally as well as emotionally. The little children were extremely susceptible to pediatric illnesses such as whooping cough, chicken pox, and the mumps, which raged through the ship like sudden fires. My father had his work cut out for him with this task and, together with the British captain and the ship's officers, was constantly busy trying to "get these people home properly," as he put it. As far as I know, he never received any recognition for this lousy job that depleted his last physical reserves.

He had very little time for me. Yet we did have a fixed date once a day. At the end of the afternoon, I'd go to the lounge where only the British ship's officers would be; they were well-fed, rosy-cheeked, and often wore short white pants. It was serene and quiet there. My father was dressed in an American military uniform, long khaki pants, and a shirt with his insignia on the collar. He smoked nonstop, lighting one Player with the next, his fingers brown with nicotine. He looked exhausted and alarmed. He was still extremely thin, as he had been a few months earlier on the bridge over the Cideng Canal.

We were sitting at the bar. "How is your mother doing?" he asked occasionally. "Fine," I'd answer.

But I didn't want to converse. I just wanted to sit there with my head against his shoulder and not talk about anything, not about my mother, not about the camps, and not about Holland.

Every day they gave me a glass of tomato juice, and every day my father would ask: "Would you like some pepper with that? It's very good," and then he'd pick up the canister and thoughtfully and carefully sprinkle the white kernels in the glass. I knew it wouldn't last more than half an hour, but I wished that it would never end.

Chapter 16

HOLLAND

We alter the past to become part of it and to make it our own.
　　　　　—David Lowenthal, *The Past Is a Foreign Country*

On a misty morning in March 1946 after a four-week journey, the *Alcantara* docked in the English port of Southampton. I was hanging over the railing and to my disbelief and amazement saw English longshoremen, white men, in shabby work clothes, tugging at and hauling cables. I had never seen a European perform any physical labor. I couldn't believe my eyes.

That afternoon a Dutch ship, whose name I don't recall, brought us from England to Amsterdam.

My grandparents in Wassenaar welcomed us. Their house was located on the edge of the dunes, right near the Duindigt racetrack. The heater was whirring. Everyone was kind.

Many things were strange. It still froze at night, and in the morning there would be white frost on the ground and on the tree branches, a marvelous spectacle that I still enjoy every time it occurs. Just as I still find pleasure in the changing of the seasons. You have to be born in the tropics to really experience and appreciate the special quality of that.

At night my grandmother would put a cup of water outside on the balcony and show it to me the next morning. It was ice. I was dumbstruck.

A few days later I entered sixth grade. Everyone in this little village school was very nice as well. Sometimes you hear a complaint from people who came to the Netherlands after the war: "We didn't find any audience for what we experienced during the war in the Indies." The reproach is that "we couldn't share our story."

Those first few weeks I always found a willing ear among the Dutch for my camp years, although they could also jabber on endlessly about their hunger winter.

I just didn't feel like talking about the war years and the camps very often. Not because I was left with a trauma but simply because I had other things on my mind—girls, playing soccer, going skating—that were far more interesting to me.

I soon discovered an effective method to get away from the topic. "Oh well," I'd say when someone asked me about the camps, "I rather liked it. We had no school, we wore no shoes, and our parents weren't there either. What more can you ask for?"

I still think with gratitude of the efforts the Netherlands—itself destroyed by the Germans and left penniless by the war—made on behalf of us repatriates. After all, on our way to the "fatherland" we had been taken ashore in Ataka, a hamlet somewhere near the Suez Canal. A little railway took us through the desert to a hangar decorated with small flags. A little orchestra of Italian POWs, thrilled to have made it through the war unscathed, was playing happy tunes. They had tea, chocolate milk, and oranges for us. Subsequently the Dutch government provided us with all new clothes. They gave us underwear, towels, handkerchiefs, pajamas, socks, shirts, outerwear, a winter coat, and shoes, which I hadn't worn in years. Everything free of charge.

The boys each received a cap as well. We didn't care much for that and refused to put them on. Fortunately, there was a gale in the Gulf of Biscay so that our caps soon blew overboard.

Once in Holland the entire family received double ration coupons, an enormous luxury.

For years I slept under a blanket with a woven text that read "The Netherlands helps the Indies." It was given to us by a foundation of the same name. Prewar quality. Offered to us just like that.

In the summer of 1946 I had to take an entrance exam for the Rijnlands Lyceum[9] in Wassenaar. And I actually passed it! I can't prove it, but I strongly suspect that those teachers and other school authorities covered my results with a huge cloak of charity. It's almost impossible that I made it through on my own steam. After all, I hadn't had any regular education in years.

One December night in 1946 my mother tucked me in. At the time we were living in an abandoned house of NSB people[10] who were now in prison. While it stood empty, all the windows had been smashed, which was not all that bad in the summer but in the fall they were covered with pieces of cardboard. It barely kept the chilly wind out of my room.

My mother tightened the blankets around me, plumped up my pillow, and said, "Do you still remember that Sone? They shot him."

She kissed me good-night, turned off the light, and left the room.

I lay there in the dark, wide awake, miserable and struggling with feelings of grief and horror.

That is, I believe, where my later desire began to find out what happened in the Dutch East Indies during the Pacific War. Afterward, I also did research on who Lieutenant Kenichi Sone really was.

From the Japanese Embassy in The Hague and the Ministry of Health and Welfare in Tokyo I obtained the address of his widow. I wrote her a letter and asked whether she would mind telling me about her husband. I found a Japanese woman who was willing to translate my letter. Half a year later the response from Sone's widow arrived.

---

9. The Dutch secondary school system had, and still has, different paths. The *lyceum*, as elsewhere in Europe, is one of the more academically oriented high schools.

10. NSB: the Nationaal Socialistische Beweging, the Dutch Nazi party made up of collaborators with the enemy.

In 1942 Sone was thirty-two years old. He was born near Osaka. It is possible that he was a Christian, as many in that region are. During his imprisonment in Batavia in 1946 he received many letters from friends. His correspondence with them and with his family members in Japan is kept in the National Archives in The Hague. I read this. In a letter to a friend he mentions with some pleasure that one of his colleagues gave him a Bible. From a letter to his brother one gathers that he had a young son.

He studied at a trade school (a kind of secondary school?) where he learned English, among other things. He completed his military service in Japan and left it as a reserve second lieutenant. He went to work at the office of the shipping company where his father probably had served as merchant marine officer. In 1939 he was ordered back into military service. In 1942 he was sent to Java. He probably did have a small son. On Java he was named commander of the POW camp the 10th Battalion in Batavia, where he ran a very severe and harsh regime with many beatings and other corporal punishments.

My father was the oldest officer there, and the highest ranking one among the prisoners, which is why he had frequent contact with Sone. Did this lead to a certain familiarity despite themselves and despite the difference in their ages? Did they talk about their sons?

In April 1944 Sone became the commander of the women's camp Cideng. When my father heard about that transfer, did he ask Sone to look after his wife and children? I don't know. My father never spoke about it and I never asked.

Where did Sone's concern for me come from? Was I a substitute for a little son in Japan? I don't know.

In June 1945 he was promoted to captain and a few days later transferred to Bandung, where he was later arrested by the British troops and taken to Batavia.

In Cideng, too, Sone was a harsh and cruel commander. The report of the court of justice and the text of his sentence are clear about that. He made a profound impression with his savage, rapidly appearing and disappearing outbursts of rage. It would happen, after such an outburst, that he would distribute cigarettes and chocolate and then go downtown calmly and properly dressed. He was often drunk.

In the final six months of the war his rages grew worse. According to some of his colleagues he was manic-depressive. On 5, 6, and 7 June 1945 and once again on 21 and 22 June he punished the camp collectively for having smuggled food through the fence: the camp was not given any food during those days, a cruel penalty for hungry women and children. In addition he had the heads shaved of some ten women who were directly involved.

That period in Cideng had become extremely unpleasant, to put it euphemistically. The food kept decreasing and deteriorating. Hunger raged; the camp grew filthier and more crowded because more and more women from other camps were being moved in. The cesspools overflowed; there was a huge lack of medications and there was only one hour of water a day. But Cideng was not a "concentration camp" as some call it with an eagerness that I do not care for at all.

Moreover, the entire control consisted of a lieutenant, a sergeant, two Korean corporals, one of whom is praised for his humanity, eleven Japanese soldiers, and twelve heihos armed with wooden rifles, who became very skittish whenever the commander came anywhere near them.

Sone was tried by a temporary Dutch court-martial. After a long trial with a decidedly weak Japanese defender, with many misinterpretations and rather sloppy testimonies, he was sentenced to death on 6 September 1946. He was found guilty of war crimes of systematic terror and ruthless treatment of POWs and civilian internees. His superiors, not he, were accused of the deficient distribution of food and medications. The text and phraseology of the sentence have a vindictive undertone.

On 7 December 1946 he was executed by a firing squad in a narrow passage off the Glodok Prison yard in Batavia.

Captain Sone bows in the Japanese manner for the court-martial.

Aerial photo of Glodok Prison in Batavia, where Sone was imprisoned during the trial. In one of the corridors between the buildings, he was executed by a firing squad on December 7, 1946, and summarily buried. Glodok Prison was demolished in 1982.

Sone abused many people, terrorized them and caused them misfortune and despair. He deserved to be punished. But I cannot shake the uncomfortable feeling that this death sentence was a case of victor's justice.

In 1946 I had no inkling of any of this.

I enjoyed the lovely Dutch seasons, the flowering plants and the hawthorns in springtime, the smell of hay drying in the meadows, roaming around in and exploring the dunes, the fresh Atlantic breeze at the beach of the Wassenaarse Slag, and later the snow, sledding, and skating on the frozen ponds of Oud Wassenaar Castle.

Afterword

Our family moved to Amsterdam in August 1947 because my father had found a job there. My secondary school years were relaxed, after which I did my university studies at what was then still known as the Gemeente Universiteit (Municipal University). I continued to live and work in Amsterdam, the war and the camp years rarely in my thoughts, since I was too busy with other things, such as my family and my profession.

One fall afternoon in 1976 I was riding my bike through the underpass of the Rijksmuseum and saw there was a small exhibit about the Japanese internment camps, and on the spur of the moment I went in. There were documents, letters that had been saved, Japanese paper money, the numbers of camp internees, bracelets, wooden sandals, tin plates, and frequently mended garments. Seeing the objects again touched and deeply affected me.

From that day on I became absorbed in the history of colonialism and Asia, especially that of the contemporary period. In addition, I read large amounts of camp and war reminiscences, a genre that provided me with a number of surprises.

The first surprise was that there was not just a little but, quite the contrary, a great deal of literature about the Japanese era in the Dutch East Indies. No one could insist that there is no interest in it, as is so often claimed. Diaries, novels, scientific studies, lectures, memoirs, essays, autobiographies, whatever you want. Shelf after overflowing shelf, dozens of meters long, an interminable quantity, a *banjir*, a veritable deluge. Every bookstore that is up to date has a separate department about the occupation, the internment, and the decolonization of Indonesia. Whoever complains that interest in the subject is lacking has no idea what he is talking about or else has never entered a bookstore or a library.

The second surprise was that virtually all of these sources turned out to deal almost exclusively with the European section of the colonial population of the Indies, which in 1942 numbered over a hundred thousand individuals. Thus, this group was the size of a small provincial Dutch town.

It was truly embarrassing to discover that there is hardly any attention paid to the fate of those who remained outside the camps. These were primarily Eurasian Dutch people, known as Indos, which formed a far larger group than the totoks, the full-blooded Europeans.

For the Indos the years of the Japanese occupation as well as the postwar years were dreadful. The Japanese, and often the Indonesians as well, mistrusted them and treated them with contempt. In the course of 1944, life outside the camps became extremely painful for them. There were desperate Indo women who sought protection and attempted to acquire the status of *belanda,* European, in order to gain entrance into the internment camps. Such women weren't always welcome and were sometimes referred to as "kampung chickens."

After the Japanese capitulation the Indos encountered even more difficult times, suffering the rage and bloodthirstiness in the revolutionary period of the pemudas, at whose mercy they had been helplessly delivered because nobody was concerned about protecting them.

They were the real victims of the war in the Indies: they lost their social position, their property, their income, their motherland, their history, and their future.

But that isn't all. Hard to believe as it is, in almost all the texts the indigenous population receives even less attention than the Indos. During the Japanese occupation two and a half million Javanese died of starvation and deprivation. The population's health reached rock bottom, and the economy was wrecked, as everything was put into the service of the Japanese war effort.

More than four hundred thousand *romushas,* the native laborers who had been recruited by the Japanese army, lost their lives in the construction of airports and railways. They had absolutely no rights and were dying like flies, but you never hear anything about them and can rarely find anything to read about their fate and suffering.

Unfortunately, the Indies Monument in The Hague exudes some of the same atmosphere. The figures in the monument could really be part of almost any war monument; not a single one of the thirteen figures has anything specifically Indonesian or Asian in facial expression, posture, or dress. I find this lamentable. After all, those poor natives—*tanis* (farmers), romushas, and becak drivers—were Dutch subjects too.

Not until the more recent years has any attention been paid to the "outside-campers," but interest in the fate of the indigenous population during the Japanese occupation is still almost negligible.

The third surprise was (and is) the quality of what has been written, or rather the lack of it. I actually recognized very little. As a rule the "Jap camp" was described as a three-and-a-half-year-long road of suffering, hunger, humiliation, and barbarism. But I recalled it as a fairly carefree and sometimes adventurous period.

Usually there's nothing but self-pity, indignation, racist ill will, and a total preoccupation with one's own suffering. Rudy Kousbroek already pointed this out as early as 1971, and since then not much has changed, although there are exceptions.

When reading the literature about the Pacific War, you get the feeling that if you were there you ought to feel like a victim. Apparently, the war victim status is a highly desirable one. It seems as if it is indecent to speak about the Japanese occupation and internment in simple, sober terms. One quickly gets the impression that imperialism, aggression, and cruelty are twentieth-century Asian discoveries made by inferior, mentally disturbed Japanese who invaded our own Indies where they had no business being.

There are a number of associations that continue to make every effort to accentuate this one-sided image in public opinion. I'm referring, for example, to the Stichting Japanse Ereschulden (Foundation for Japanese Debts of Honor), which doesn't deal with honor as much as it does with cash, and continues to ask the Japanese for apologies and money as compensation for the suffering endured. Furthermore, in the colonial context the concept "debt of honor" is pretty distressing. The phrase was coined, after all, in 1899 by Van Deventer, who in an article in the journal *Gids* (Guide) denounced the Dutch exploitation and extortion of the East Indies.

What I find downright shameful is that they base their claim of $20,000 on the fate of the American citizens of Japanese origin who were interned and treated with contempt in camps in California and other western states in 1942. More than forty years later the American government, apologizing profusely, awarded them this sum in compensation for what had been done to them by their own administration.

There is also the Stichting Jongens in de Japanse Kampen '42–'45 (Foundation for Boys from the Japanese Camps '42–'45), which in its public statements keeps hammering away at the apologies that the Japanese government should offer, although this was already done by the previous emperor, the new emperor, prime ministers, and ambassadors.

Furthermore, they completely skip over the Yoshida-Stikker Protocol of 1956 in which the Netherlands relinquished any claims. No attempt at historical analysis or reconciliation is ever, *ever* made in their society's newspaper. It is always filled with pieces written in vulgar language where the Pacific War is waged all over again with, of course, the writer as moral victor who always is too clever for the "Japs."

Finally, there is the Vereniging van Kinderen uit de Japanse Bezetting en Bersiap (Association of Children of the Japanese Occupation and the Bersiap). Its members are those who lived through the Japanese occupation as young children or heard about it secondhand. Reading their paper will make you fall over with embarrassment and disbelief. All their subsequent troubles, I repeat, *all* their subsequent troubles, existential or not, are traced back to those three years of internment. Having been held back in school, dropping out of college, a failed career, being left by their partner (fed up with all the complaining), impotence: no matter what they dream up, it is all blamed on their camp experiences. Some of them were mere babies or newborns at the time.

The true victims—and they most certainly do exist—don't beat the drum this way and aren't looking for conspicuous publicity. Of course, there are associations, too, such as the Stichting Pelita (Pelita Foundation), that do their work for this category of people in a quiet and professional manner.

I have written and spoken about the failed, one-sided, and sterile processing of the war experiences in the Dutch East Indies, and I have thereby not minced any words. I am frequently blamed for having said something unacceptable. I am accused of a "lack of solidarity" and even of "collaboration" (albeit after the fact). It has even been argued that opinions like mine indicate repression and therefore show explicit proof of a serious war trauma. Well, sure, one can keep going on like this forever.

Face-to-face in occasional encounters I often do get approval, but in public opinion the image of those horrific "Jap camps" is almost ineradicable. It's as if the image of the sadistic "Jap" who delighted daily in humiliating and torturing Dutch men and women is a deeply cherished one.

I will not be party to that.

Appendix

THE QUESTIONNAIRE

Introduction: Why I Filled in This Questionnaire

After the capitulation of Japan in August 1945, many Dutch nationals departed for the Netherlands. The first immigration wave from the colony, which took place from the end of 1945 into 1946, consisted primarily of totoks, Dutch people who hadn't gone to the Indies to settle but to practice a trade or a profession. They went to Holland either for a "recuperation leave," as it was called, or to return to the homeland definitively. On the whole, they were warmly welcomed and received by family members who lived in the Netherlands. Pleasant as that may have been, among the general public in Holland there was no interest whatsoever in what had happened in Asia during the Second World War. However, the newcomers were inundated with stories about the so-called hunger winter of 1944, and the resistance against the Germans, in which just about everyone claimed to have participated. In reaction, the immigrants couldn't help, first of all, emphasizing that over there in the tropics a real war had been waged and a real occupation had occurred. A second reaction was the constant plea for recognition of the acts of war and the suffering that had been endured. These two aspects remain typical of the camp literature that was published after the war. Its nature is one of affronted rage. What appeared were titles like *De gele terreur* (The yellow terror, 1946) and *De lach uit leed geboren: Herinneringen uit de Japanse concentratiekampen voor vrouwen en kinderen* (The smile born of suffering: Memories from the Japanese concentration camps for women and children, 1971).

The first general characteristic of this genre is a vindictive, indignant, and sometimes almost racist tone. "The Japs treated us like coolies," they say without a trace of embarrassment. The total lack of humor or irony is remarkable. The black-and-white picture the authors present is one of three and a half years of uninterrupted humiliation and starvation in a camp existence replete with sadistic Japs who tortured and decapitated merely for their own pleasure. The attention is paid exclusively to personal suffering without any interest in the fate of other groups of the population, such as the native peoples, or the Eurasians "outside the camps," those who were not interned. Two elements invariably emerge: first of all, the Japanese interest in young European women; you would almost think that they had embarked on their southern campaign not for the oil but for the women. In the second place, that there is no recognition in the Netherlands, as mentioned above, for the disaster endured in the Indies. Moreover, that complaint is still alive and kicking today. Noteworthy, too, is an almost obsessive endeavor to have the camps be similar to the KZLager, the Nazi concentration camps. These became the paradigm, including, or perhaps even thanks to, all the horrific connotations.

I call this genre the KZ-genre. Over the course of the years there isn't a trace of maturation to be found in this genre. The flow of these kinds of publications relentlessly continues, and their quality remains dreadful. Apparently there is a market for *Gruselmärchen,* horror stories, about sadistic slant-eyes and *kenpeitai,* Japanese military police, brutes.

The second immigration wave (1950–56) consisted mainly of Eurasians fleeing the land of their birth because they were being discriminated against and felt unsafe and unwanted in the new Indonesia. This group of victims had literally lost everything during or as a result of the war and arrived in the Netherlands uprooted and desperate. They were not warmly welcomed by family members because they didn't have any there. What they did encounter, however, was the same treatment of indifference that the totoks had run into a few years before. It is understandable that they embraced the set model—the KZ-genre—for their own stories.

Next, the version that dissented from the KZ-genre in the literature was just barely assertive in tone. I call this a genre of benign perspective. It is characterized by a calm, sometimes ironic tone without any self-pity or victimization. Titles were published such as Rob Nieuwenhuis's *Een beetje oorlog* (A little bit of war, 1979) and Ernest Hillen's *The Way of a Boy: A Memoir of Java*, 1993. The narrative style is diametrically opposed to that of the shrill, sensational tone of the KZ-genre.

Publications of both genres simply continued on throughout the years, as if they had nothing to do with each other or—what is more likely—didn't want to have anything to do with each other. The "war memories" disappeared from the public interest, with the exception of some social and political wrangling about Emperor Hirohito's visit to the Netherlands in 1971 and Queen Beatrix's aborted plan to visit Japan in 1986. But this had already begun to change in the early 1980s.

In 1981 the book *Bezonken rood* (*Sunken Red*) by Jeroen Brouwers appeared, which takes place in Cideng, the notorious women's camp in what was then Batavia (today's Jakarta). Although Brouwers doesn't actually call it a concentration camp, he does describe it as if it were a Nazi camp. Cideng is presented as a real German concentration camp: guard towers with machine guns, searchlights, and electrified barbed wire, ghastly cruelties during roll call inflicted by guards in heavy boots with whips and dogs, just like the SS. Brouwers himself calls the book autobiographic fiction, which is certainly allowed. However, he wraps it up in a historical truth that can be checked. For instance, by yours truly who himself was in Cideng from August 1943 until October 1944. And who knows that what Brouwers writes are inventions and lies, aimed at sensational representation and rabble-rousing. And he succeeds, for the book enjoyed many editions. But it is a delusion, nevertheless.

Be that as it may, the book made a deep impression on public opinion and thus in a very short time monopolized the KZ-genre. This image caught on in the public domain and—what is worse—was unquestioningly accepted by the press and actually treated with some enthusiasm. The far less assertive genre of the "benign perspective" received much less response.

As if this wasn't enough, in March 1994 the Foundation for Japanese Debts of Honor (Stichting Japanse Ereschulden), abbreviated to JES, was established. According to the website, its purpose is threefold: 1. Acknowledgment of guilt by the Japanese government, 2. Expression of regret over the Dutch victims by the Japanese government, and 3. Compensation (i.e., money) to the Dutch victims for the suffering endured as a result of the Japanese occupation. Points 1 and 2 have been met several times by the prime minister, as well as by the former and the new emperors. Point 3 is a different story. Under Legal Actions, the website reads: "On 30 March 2004, the Japanese Supreme Court declared itself not receptive to the appeal. Human rights were violated by the imperial military forces and, according to The Hague convention of 1907, Japan would be required to disburse compensation. The treaties signed (San Francisco Peace Treaty of 1951 and the Yoshida-Stikker Accord of 1956) prevent this." "The JES now directs itself to the moral responsibility of Japan," so the website continues. The decision by the Supreme Court of Japan will astonish no one who has even a grain of judicial instinct and, furthermore, I wonder how the JES will deal with the new objective. It now becomes clear, however, that the JES has added another objective: defending the KZ-genre by fire and sword. Those who want to qualify matters, correct certain things, or note a historical error in texts written along the line of the KZ-genre, are fiercely attacked as if (after the fact) they are collaborators and as if they are threatening an especially cherished gem of the JES. Moreover, the strange thing is that when these self-appointed representatives of "Indies society" are confronted with a slightly more nuanced picture of the Japanese occupation, they don't consider themselves fortunate or relieved that the reality didn't consist of horrors alone (Hooray, it was different from what we thought), but, foaming at the mouth with rage, they carry on like madmen against anyone who dares to qualify a bit.

My criticism of the argumentation, motives, and opinions of the JES can be found in my the Afterword to my memoir *"Voor Fredje is het kamp een paradijs"* and in the following piece, "The Questionnaire." To go up against the KZ-genre is to fight a losing battle, for it is far too popular. Apparently, people are deeply attached to the state of victimization.

For the sake of doing at least something, I applied for the form of the JES questionnaire and completed it truthfully.

The Questionnaire

Foundation for Japanese Debts of Honor
Secretariat: P. Valmontkade 716, 2510 JK The Hague
Registered with the KVK in The Hague under reg. no. ZI I O I J J
WAR INDEMNITY CLAIM FORM
Form to be completed in print or typed

Question 1. Victim's family name/victim's first name

Ladies and Gentlemen, what a good idea. I will complete this form because money is always useful, especially a sum of twenty thousand dollars, and I wouldn't want to miss this chance. Let those Japanese pay the price for what they made us suffer. Although it's quite a long time ago. Until recently I really didn't pay much attention to the Pacific War. That was fifty years ago. I was a child at the time. I was living in the Dutch East Indies. I can assure you that growing up as a European child in a colonial society is quite a pleasant experience. I had a happy childhood even though that world was inevitably on its way to a fateful destiny: war, revolution, destruction. But, as you can understand, at the time I didn't know that yet. I was repatriated, as they then called it, in 1946.

In Holland, too, I had a happy life. I finished secondary school, found a job at the town clerk's office, started a family. So, all of it quite ordinary.

The war was an incident. I never thought about it anymore. When I began to complete your form, I had to dig down very deeply into my memory. Of course, I know about the Pacific War. After all, I lived through it myself as a boy. But I need not be told how fragmentary, subjective, and untrustworthy memory can be. The more I delved into your questions, the greater my confusion.

Guess what, I thought, I had better read up on what's been written about this period by people who really know. Well, in that attempt I ran into a few surprises.

The first was that there isn't too little but an amazingly large amount of literature on the Japanese era in the Dutch East Indies. Diaries, novels, scientific treatises, memoirs, essays, autobiographies, you name it, shelf after shelf after shelf, dozens and dozens of feet long, an interminable quantity, a banjir, a deluge. Every up-to-date bookstore actually has a separate section about the occupation, the internment, and the decolonization of Indonesia.

Thus, attention galore.

The second surprise was that all these sources turned out to deal almost entirely with the European population alone. And that group was as large, or more precisely as small, as the population of a provincial town in Holland. What a luxury!

Imagine if the war history of Emmen or Naarden were to take up this much space on the shelves of a bookstore. How jealous the other towns would be.

I didn't study, Ladies and Gentlemen, and I didn't choose my literature very systematically, nor did I approach it very methodically. I read what I happened to find on the shelf in the library and bookstore. However, I did profit a great deal by responding to your questions. I will frequently quote facts and formulations verbatim from others, as for instance from Mr. Joop Al. This is not a scientific argument, so I won't provide any footnotes or bibliographic references. I can justify every sentence, should you so desire. As a civil servant I have learned to carefully note down all sources. If you wish, I will send you a list of the books I have read.

The third surprise was the quality of the writing. It really fell short of any expectations. I came upon stories that over the years have grown steadily more horrific. There is the phenomenon that in the interim some of the survivors of the Japanese camps have acquired the status of sacrosanct war victim, in their environment, in their family, often among those who themselves had never known the Indies. The weak point, I quickly noticed, is that much of what has been written about the Japanese occupation is an exclusive preoccupation with one's own fate and one's personal suffering.

Ladies and Gentlemen, it is strange, but I remember things very differently from much of what those writings contain. Only in some of the diaries by little boys like myself—I was ten, twelve years old during the occupation—did I recognize some truth of what I, too, had experienced. As I see it, these diaries are extremely reliable because, after all, the boys were simply writing down what they were experiencing. And, just like me, they really lived it with eyes wide open.

Your first question asks for the name of "the victim." Initially I thought: What now? This form is not meant for me. But some time later, when I had familiarized myself a little with the literature and the terminology it used, I got it.

In reading about the Pacific War you gradually get the feeling that you ought to feel like a victim, that this is the normal reaction. Surreptitiously I'm thinking: Me, a victim?

No, not at all. It simply had to do with war. Not always fun but neither was it all that bad, and at times actually exciting. I wouldn't have wanted to miss it. In the meantime, however, you don't dare say that openly anymore. You can't help feeling that it is almost indecent to speak simply and matter-of-factly about the Japanese occupation and the internment. You get the impression fairly quickly that imperialism, war, and brutalities were twentieth-century Asian inventions discovered by retarded, mentally disturbed Japanese who had invaded our own Indies where they had no business.

There is another thing you run into quite often. "In the Netherlands there is hardly any interest in all we lived through during the war," it says. "We didn't have an outlet for our story," it says accusingly. I don't understand this.

In Holland in 1946 they gave us double ration coupons for the entire family for months on end. Double coupons! No one objected to it, which was also very kind.

On the trip back to the Netherlands, in Ataka, a small town near the Suez Canal, the Dutch government provided us with all kinds of new clothing. Free of charge we received underwear, handkerchiefs, pajamas, socks, shirts, outerwear, an overcoat, a cap, shoes. Shoes! I hadn't worn those in years.

The Dutch government had established a welcome center in the middle of the Egyptian desert, where they served tea and candy, and handed out rolls and oranges in the festively decorated barracks. A small orchestra of cheerful Italian prisoners of war, thrilled that the war was over, intensified the joyful mood with happy music while winking at the girls. They were nice guys.

Even today I still sleep under a blanket that has "The Netherlands helps the Indies" woven into it. Prewar quality! Given to us just like that.

No attention? No interest?

My Dutch classmates were always interested in my camp experiences, to which I'd add a layer or two. They ate it up. In comparison their drivel about the hunger winter was nothing.

Apparently, the status of being a war victim is an extremely desirable one. In fact, Ladies and Gentlemen, I discovered that there is actually an association. It is called VBJJ or something like that. The members lived through the Japanese occupation at a young age or had the experience second- or even thirdhand. When you read their club's newsletter, you are overcome with embarrassment and disbelief. All their subsequent troubles, I repeat, *all* their subsequent existential troubles—not being promoted in school, failing final exams, dropping out of college, pedophilia, professional failure, being left by a partner (who got tired of listening to their whining), impotence, old age ailments, no matter what you dream up, everything is blamed on their camp experiences. Or on grandma's camp experiences.

As if those few years were that influential for the whole of their life's destiny. They call themselves "a caged child" and say: "My best years were taken away from me by the Japs." They are pitiful. They are victims.

Ladies and Gentlemen, I do not belong to this club.

You will find my first and last name at the bottom of this form.

Question 2. Residence of the victim on 7 December 1941?

I—that is to say "the victim"—was living in Batavia.

It was still a small city at the time. As a child, I had no inkling of the colonial society. I was at home in the country and among its people. I knew nothing else.

Not until I became involved with your claim form, which made me reflect upon that period, did I begin to wonder: By what right were the Dutch actually there? Weren't we simply foreign occupiers who neglected the population and exploited the land for financial profit?

I once read somewhere that in 1942 in Indonesia there were only 221 Indonesian physicians and 230 academics out of a population of 60 million. I am not proud of that.

But neither do I feel guilty about it. This is history; it is what happened. Just imagine that we, you and I, should have to pay an indemnity fee—because of a debt of honor—to those people. All those wars and expeditions by the KNIL; I don't even want to think about it.

Speaking of the KNIL. It collapsed dishonorably and bloodlessly in March 1942. It was unceremoniously destroyed in eight days. *Berani mati,* dare to die, was the KNIL's motto. I only saw them wave white rags. That is disappointing to a small boy. No heroism, no desperate offensive, no valiant soldierly stunts. The Japanese 16th Imperial Army was another cup of tea. It was very different from the shaky rebels and the starving kampung population, the adversaries of yore when the Dutch East Indies was being "pacified."

Question 3. Victim's date of birth

I was born in January 1933. So I was nine years old when the war started in our area. And I was twelve when it suddenly stopped.

I had a clear look, keen eyes, and, even if I say so myself, an independent spirit. The latter was caused, of course, by not having had any schooling for several years.

Question 4. In which countries was the victim held prisoner?

Well, how am I to respond to this question? In the Dutch East Indies? Or should I say in Indonesia? Or is it realistic to say in the Japanese East Indies?

I was a prisoner on Java.

Question 5. Where was the victim first interned?

That word again!

Internment began in September 1942 in Batavia. My father was a prisoner of war in Bandung. My mother, my sister, and I were housed in the Kramat district.

In 1942 the urban climate had grown more dangerous for Europeans, and the camps offered protection. The Japanese called it *tempat perlindungan,* a protected area. And that was true. It was considered to be safer in the camps than outside. The threat didn't come from the Japanese. The invading troops conducted themselves with discipline. It was not a disorderly army; the soldiers were calm and quiet.

Kramat was located on the edge of the city. It was a real Indies tempo dulu district with spacious, cool colonial houses surrounded by large gardens. The streets and avenues were shaded by tall kenari trees from which tasty nuts would drop. There were babus, female nursemaids and house servants. On the weekends we were allowed to leave the camp. It was a carefree time. The only annoying thing was that the women had organized schooling, which interrupted our playing in the street: roller-skating, marbles, softball, making small fires.

A year later we were transferred to Camp Cideng. We were transported in a long line of cheerfully ringing becaks, pedicabs.

Cideng was in another section of Batavia next to the railroad. It had been built more recently than Kramat. The houses and gardens were smaller, and the stately avenues were missing. The camp was more crowded than Kramat. Other than that, life wasn't bad, at least as long as I was there. We no longer had servants, but we still had pets. We weren't hungry. My mother earned some extra money by making and selling candy. Fortunately, we had no school, and we could play outside all day long as much as we wanted. There were a lot of children.

It seems that later on there may have been electrified barbed wire, guard towers, and machine guns. At least, there's a book about that. I know the writer of that book, Jeroentje, a somewhat fat, foolish little boy of three who always wanted to be part of the big boys' group. We called him Silly Jeroentje. He described it all in great detail. He also saw and endured the most horrifying crimes and tortures: the "Jap" goes around shooting, slashing with his saber, and lashing with his whip, he writes.

I saw none of this and don't remember anything of the sort. In the postwar trials concerning this particular camp there are no records of this. Still, perhaps all of that occurred after November 1944, when I was no longer in Cideng. And those court records are, of course, incomplete and not entirely to be trusted so shortly after the war. I do wonder sometimes what purpose that barbed wire, those guard towers, and machine guns would have served. After all, it wouldn't have entered the mind of any European to dare leave the camp.

During the night the locals often barged into the camp like thieves. Apparently, there was a lot to be had for them. Might the Japanese have placed those towers and heavy weapons there to keep the natives out rather than us in? However, Ladies and Gentlemen, that is not the issue here.

In November 1944 my mother, my sister, and I were transferred to yet another camp. It was located near the small town of Tangerang, a few kilometers outside Batavia. It was an actual prison, a square building with a large inner courtyard and dormitories, shower areas, and latrines arranged in a square around it. Outside the building were fields for the cultivation of vegetables and fruit.

I hated it there. Never saw a Japanese. Three sturdy Dutch ladies ruled the boys' dormitory where they had established a Boy Scouts' system that still regularly appears in my nightmares. It was my first and last experience with a totalitarian regime. It governed our life every minute of the day and night; it insisted on penetrating every thought, every word, and every deed. There was an iron-fisted atmosphere with all kinds of bizarre rituals and countless commands and taboos, whose sense was unclear to us.

They constantly gave us sermons about purity, whose obsessive nature didn't escape us, young as we were. They set you up against each other in a false camaraderie all day long, through competitions in virtue (to such an extent that you had an almost irrepressible urge to do something "dirty") or in things over which you had no power ("Whose tomato plant grew most during the night?"). That, Ladies and Gentlemen, was suffering.

Fortunately, I turned twelve three months later, which made me a prisoner of war. How proud I was! POWs were interned in boys' or men's camps, and so, in January 1945, together with a couple of dozen other partners in adversity, I was transferred under the command of a number of kind-hearted heihos, Javanese military aides in service to the Japanese, to Cimahi, a small mountain town in the Preanger region of West Java.

That was a wise move in every way. We were growing too old for the women's camp. Although the Boy Scout approach did try to direct our thoughts—or, better put, divert them from certain things—it was a losing battle. There are circumstances embedded in our natural character that gave this effort little chance of success.

The camp was overrun with young women and growing girls. Generally, they wore shorts, so that you could see their thighs very clearly, and on top they had bodices, a cloth tied around the neck and the middle that covered the bosom but left the back bare. We quickly discovered the age-old truth that clothing often accentuates what is covered more than it conceals. And we were reaching the age when you really want to look at women as much as possible and feel like examining and touching them. With a cherubic look on our faces, we were more than delighted to accompany our mothers to the shower area. Looking without being seen! At night when we were together again in the dormitory, we would report enthusiastically on all the shapes, sizes, and forms in every stage of blossoming and decline. "Aduh, I had to cover myself very fast with my towel," my friend Kees said. And of course we laughed uproariously.

It was wise, Ladies and Gentlemen. There hadn't been any adult European men around anymore for a long time, and many of the women were longing for them. Who can blame them? We heard a lot of stories about sexual adventures and about the money that some women would pay for them, which created an atmosphere that Lord Baden-Powell surely wouldn't have anticipated. I read that a baby was actually born in Camp Cideng in April 1945.

I believe I've never left any place with a greater sense of glee. We drove away from Camp Tangerang in an open truck, and I sighed with relief, although it was raining cats and dogs and my sister was crying her eyes out.

So from January 1945 until August 1945 I was in a boys' camp, in a residential area surrounded by a bamboo fence that was a former NCO district in Cimahi, which had been a garrison town of the KNIL. There were eight boys per room, with a total of about thirty boys in the house. At night we had pillow fights. Our house was run by a calm and tolerant man whose sole aim it apparently was to steer the group of boys safely through the war. He established a few simple rules so that we would treat each other decently, but he avoided any attempt at educating us or instilling any ideals in us. That was a huge relief.

There were a few dozen other adults in our camp as well. They did organize some schooling, but we succeeded in sabotaging that quite nicely by playing hooky, coming late, and raising a ruckus. In the end they no longer had the energy to keep after us.

So we just goofed around. Sometimes we had chores to do, clean up, sweep the street, unblock gutters. Sometimes we worked on the farm in the mountains. Everyone was pretty scrawny, but the climate was marvelous. Nothing much really happened.

In August the war suddenly came to an end. On occasion I hear fellow sufferers complain: "We weren't truly liberated." Well, what did they want? A moment of reckoning? Bombings? Artillery duels? Tanks in the city and fighting in the streets? No, fortunately there was none of that.

There is a famous photograph with the caption: "Japanese soldier in the street overwhelmed with grief over the defeat." The man is sitting on the edge of the sidewalk. His tunic is half-open and saturated with dark stains, his head is lowered, his legs are spread, his boots stand beside his feet with the street trash. It was one of the first days after the liberation. I had just gone for a walk outside the camp with a few other boys.

The tunic wasn't covered in tears or sweat. It was blood. He had committed seppuku, the traditional Japanese reaction to overpowering shame. He had ripped his belly open with his short dagger.

To this day the image fills me with horror and pity. How old would that man have been? Did he have parents in Japan, friends, a beloved? Once you've seen a scene like this you can no longer have an irreconcilable attitude, because you now know there are things that go beyond all comprehension.

Food attached to parachutes came falling from the sky, and you could buy and sell anything at all at the small pasar, market, which had sprung up rather quickly beside the gate. The market women and the older men were courteous and kind, but the young Indonesians weren't exactly friendly. Red-and-white flags were flying everywhere.

And right they are, it is their country, I thought at the time. And that, Ladies and Gentlemen, is still my opinion today.

Question 6. Did the victim suffer torture, corporal punishment, or other forms of violence?

It was the early morning roll call. The boys were standing in the street in front of the house. A chilly mountain wind was blowing, and we were stamping our feet and jumping up and down to stay warm.

Roll call generally didn't amount to much. A sloppy Korean soldier would rapidly pass by on a rickety bike. It was just a tedious chore to him. We called him Dirk. We didn't have much respect for the man. "Mornin', Dirk," we often called out, and wouldn't dream of standing at attention or behaving in an orderly fashion.

That particular morning, however, it was the commander himself taking roll call. He was a twenty-two-year-old lieutenant of Japanese Korean parentage, and a decent fellow. But he was in a bad mood that day. Maybe he had heard of the merciless bombings by which in one night the Americans had reduced entire cities to ashes. Maybe he was worried about his parents or a girlfriend in one of those cities. At the time we weren't aware of that, and, had we known, it wouldn't have bothered us very much. We were dealing with simple but clear rules like: "It's your own fault" and "That's just too bad."

At roll call each person had to hand over twenty dead bedbugs a day. The Japanese were terrified of infections and vermin. The remedy was so effective that there soon was a serious shortage of bedbugs.

Dirk on his little bicycle had never paid all that much attention to it, but Lieutenant Kunimoto took it very seriously. It turned out that the boy in front of me didn't have enough dead bugs with him. Kunimoto lectured him severely, and I allowed myself a joke, saying something like: "The lieutenant thinks you're a jerk, Kees." Before I knew what was happening, I received a hard whack in the face. I was seeing stars. I hadn't been hit like that in a long time. Before the war my father would on occasion smack me like that.

From that moment on I avoided Kunimoto as much as possible.

They knew what they were doing, those Japanese. The heihos, the Indonesian military aides who were in charge of most of the surveillance of the camp, were scared to death of their Japanese superiors. To our amusement, at the approach of any officer they'd take to their heels as fast as they could. When they had stepped over the line, they were harshly beaten right in front of the gate. They had to drop their pants and were whipped with a leather belt, whereupon they had to stand at attention in the sun. One day one of them was caught exchanging the watch of an internee for some eggs and a bunch of bananas. He paid the price. He was tied to a barbed wire martingale for twenty-four hours and his back was raw.

Really tough guys, those Japanese.

Question 7. Transport under inhumane conditions?

The trip from Tangerang to Cimahi took twenty-four hours, although as the crow flies it was probably no farther than a hundred kilometers. We were crammed in third-class wooden railway cars. Fortunately, they were open so you could catch some breeze because it definitely was hot. You'd also catch the sparks spraying from the locomotive as it moved. It was as if you were being attacked by sharp little bites. It caused a great deal of hilarity. "Who would ever travel third class? That's only for locals, after all," said one of the boys who always had something cheerful to offer.

The journey took a long time because the train had to stop every few kilometers to give priority to military transports. We were then given fruit and water by the local population. The guards, who were never relieved and grew more exhausted all the time, turned a blind eye. They were glad to get a piece of the pie. We were at a standstill again. Another train was sidetracked next to us. It was a military transport. The cars were jam-packed with weaponry, pieces of equipment, backpacks, and soldiers. In the nocturnal silence you could hear the hissing of the steam locomotives, and now and then the metal sound of cars being coupled. We were standing side by side. Dead silence in both trains. We looked at them and they looked at us. The Japanese boys were just a few years older than we were. They were grubby, sweaty, dead-tired, and pallid. The Japanese warlords in Tokyo had them hauled hither and yon across the entire war theater, from Manchuria to the Solomon Islands.

"They've been in that train for four days already," the heihos told us.

Question 8. Imprisonment under inhumane conditions?

Later on, in the boys' camp we had long conversations with the heihos, they on one side of the fence and we on the other. Mostly they were extremely polite. They addressed us as sinyo, young man. They frequently wanted to exchange textiles for food. We spoke Malay. The conversations were sometimes a bit personal. They made us understand that they had gone into the service primarily to escape from the poverty in the desa. It was as if we were comrades in adversity.

They knew nothing about the state of the war. "The Nippons don't know anything either," they said. "The Nippons are desperate."

They told us about the hunger, the shortages, and the diseases among the people. We could see that for ourselves. The camp's garbage cans were emptied right in front of the camp. Toward the end of the war the number of emaciated, ulcer-covered Indonesian children, dressed in rags, groping around in the trash to find something to eat, was steadily increasing.

Question 9. Slave labor?

During the day we mostly just messed around. We played games, cards, Monopoly, Sorry, or we just lazed away the time. Sometimes we'd pick the wild spinach that grew alongside the road, and we'd catch a bird or a frog. All of it would end up in the pot, which is how we satisfied our appetite.

The camp leaders arranged it in such a way that every few days we could accompany them on chores outside the camp. There was a farm higher up in the mountains, an experimental farm from the Dutch era, known as Leuwigajah, with vast fields, farmlands, cows in the pasture, and pigs in the pen. We had to weed the vegetable beds, clean the pigpens, and take care of the animals. In the afternoon they slaughtered pigs for the garrison.

We were very keen on this. You were outside the camp—an outing in and of itself—and in the fresh air. You were given extra food, and the work wasn't exactly strenuous. We kept busy slacking off. If ever a Japanese came around to check up on us, we'd alert each other and were quick to exhibit the foolish conduct of a subordinate. "Just act like a stupid coolie," we'd tell each other, "and nothing will happen to you."

They paid you fourteen cents a day, too, which we used to conduct an active business with the heihos on the way back. We bought all kinds of candy and sweets from them. In addition, we smuggled the intestines of the slaughtered pigs into the camp, which were more than welcome in the kitchen. It actually provided the soup pot with some fat.

Question 10. *Was the victim exposed to gunfire, bombings, or other war-related dangers?*

The word *victim* is beginning to disturb me more and more.

No, not at all, not during the war. The heihos had wooden rifles. But yes, after the war it became truly dangerous. You also had to be on guard when food was dropped. The Allied pilots really enjoyed their work, and in their enthusiasm they weren't always careful. Once a crate with canned cheese, corned beef, and packages of chocolate crashed right through the roof of a nearby house. It really made us laugh; the stuff was up as high as the rafters. But you did have to pay attention, for not every parachute would open up, and then the crates and metal containers would slam left and right into the ground around you and explode. Clumps of earth, dried apricots, and condoms would go flying around your ears. Then you'd better watch out.

Later on it could really get dicey. The boys of the KNIL and the Gurkhas of the British army could be quite trigger-happy, and then the bullets would whiz around your head. Friendly fire; get out of the way, boys.

Question 11. *Intentional holding back of normal medical care, food, clothing?*

It was established in the regulations that we would be provisioned out of military supplies on the same basis as the Japanese troops. Well, that wasn't exactly generous.

Occasionally, our commander Lieutenant Kunimoto did try to get something extra for the boys' camp, but he got little appreciation from his superiors. Once he showed us the bruises he had picked up during one of those harsh refusals. Still, the smallest boys would sometimes get some milk as a supplement. Kunimoto feigned ignorance when we were provided with extra food from the outside. In exchange he received quinine from us when he was on duty and shaking with a malaria attack.

And at Christmas 1944 he had actually made sure that every internee got three hundred grams of nasi goreng, fried rice. On New Year's Eve you'd actually have oliebollen, the traditional Dutch beignets. You soon discovered that it takes all kinds, many more than you had ever suspected. The kitchen help was always obscenely fat. They stole from the extra food provided for those on duty. There were a number of people among the nursing staff who terrorized the rest. Rumor had it that they hogged the extra food meant for the patients, and that they had swiped wedding bands and gold teeth of the dead. They were in great shape.

Question 12. Did the victim suffer from any diseases? Name them.

In the camp we had the same diseases from which the native population traditionally suffered. It was annoying, but we didn't think it was terrible. It seemed to be part and parcel of the situation.

Name them: There was beriberi, which made your legs swell up. It was caused by vitamin deficiency, avitaminosis. The Eurasian boys who were there also knew it from experience. They showed us a simple remedy. Along the road grew a little wild shrub, the small fiery cabe rawit, bright red chili peppers, no more than two centimeters long. They cause blisters on the skin. But when you have a vitamin deficiency, you can eat them like candy because they're loaded with vitamins. When your tongue begins to burn again, you know your deficiency is taken care of, as is the beriberi.

Then there was dysentery. The bloody, watery poop would spurt from your body, often twenty times a day. It made you very weak. Everyone had it. The guards, too, suffered from it. "Sinyo," they'd say, "we always have the runs."

There were wounds and cuts that would get infected very fast. The red line of blood poisoning would then creep up your thigh to your groin. Before you even knew it you'd have a silver dollar-sized wound on your foot that simply wouldn't heal. They were known as coolie sores. After the war they healed rapidly, at least ours did.

Other than that, there is little to report. Just as many people died in the kampung as usual.

> *Question 13. Report to what sadistic treatments the victim was subjected.*

I repeat: I do not feel like a victim.

In the course of the year 1944, life outside the camp became extremely unpleasant. There were desperate Eurasian women who sought protection, and at this stage in the game still managed to obtain the status of *belanda,* European, so that they could be included in the camps. One day a few of these outcasts came into the camp. "What are these kampung chickens doing here?" a robust blonde woman called out. I was there and, aware of what was going on, felt embarrassed. I couldn't verbalize it until later: that was the day I realized that cruelty takes many forms.

> *Question 14. If necessary provide other data.*

I do not intend to provide my bank account number.

In the first place because you will never get the amount of twenty thousand dollars, your so-called "debt of honor," and in the second place—and for this reason in particular—because I do not want to receive this money.

The Japanese aren't crazy. In 1941 you already thought they weren't all there. You were wrong then, too.

If there is anyone who has the right to financial retribution, I can list many other possibilities. The Chinese, for instance. It was in China that the Japanese truly wreaked havoc. Or the Koreans, who were occupied not for a mere three and a half years but for fifty years.

Has no one in your organization ever heard of the Yoshida-Stikker Agreement and the Protocol of 13 March 1956? Article III reads as follows: *The government of the Kingdom of the Netherlands confirms that neither itself nor any Netherlands nationals will raise against the Government of Japan any claim concerning the suffering inflicted during the Second World War by agencies of the Government of Japan upon Netherlands nationals.*

Peace with Japan was concluded in 1954.

The great political scoundrels were tried, sentenced, and executed by the International Military Tribune in Tokyo. The lesser scoundrels—from generals to sergeants—were tried in Indonesia itself. In its existence from 1946 to 1949 the Temporary Court-Martial in Jakarta tried 362 Japanese, of whom 66 were given the death penalty. Fifty-nine of them were executed.

Ladies and Gentlemen, is that not sufficient retribution? How many German military were tried and condemned to death in the Netherlands after the war? You are demanding twenty thousand US dollars per "victim" from the Japanese government as an indemnity payment. You base this sum on the indemnity payment that Japanese American citizens recently received from their own American government for the injustice they suffered at the hands of their own administration in California and other western states in 1942–45. I find this comparison indecent and inappropriate. It fills me with shame. The Japanese Americans were citizens who were interned on illegal grounds by their own government.

Nor do I wish to receive any apologies from the emperor or his successor, or from the Japanese government.

Nor do I wish to offer apologies or have apologies offered on my behalf. Not for the creation of the concentration camp *avant la lettre* in Boven Digul, New Guinea; not for the Java War; not for the destruction of Aceh in North Sumatra; not for the Bali expeditions; not for the Lombok War, not for Operation Product in 1947 or for Operation Kraai in 1948, no matter how bloody. Political actions.

No fuss. War is war.

What is it that is so special about the Dutch who were interned in the Indies? Why should "we" demand any money or apologies? In times of war people suffer starvation and deprivation. They are exposed to insecurity and hardships, they are imprisoned and separated from those they love, and they die. So what, Ladies and Gentlemen?

During the Japanese occupation two and a half million Javanese died. In the construction of airports and railways more than two hundred thousand *romushas,* local workers recruited by the Japanese army, lost their lives. During the Japanese occupation the Javanese population decreased by 20 percent.

All of them were Dutch subjects.

In all those miles of self-pitying literature you almost never hear anything about that. This concerns me deeply in completing this indemnity claim form. It offends me. It is as if my sense of honor is being attacked.

I hereby authorize the Foundation of Japanese Honorary Debts to submit to the United Nations an indemnity claim on my behalf at the expense of the Japanese government.

No, Ladies and Gentlemen, I do not authorize this.

I am not a victim. I find your claim disgraceful. Actually, I want nothing to do with you or your foundation. My honor lies in testifying truthfully to a confusing and unforgettable period.

I have my own bone to pick with the Pacific War.

At night we were on guard duty in the camp. We were instructed to forcefully call out a specific formula when inspected by a Japanese officer. I now address this formula to you: *Fukumucho ijo arimasen.* In other words: Nothing special to report.

Glossary

adat	custom, tradition
aduh	My goodness! Wow!
anglo	brazier
arang	charcoal
atap	roof, roofing (here, of dried palm fronds)
awas	watch out, be careful
babu	female house-servant
banjir	flood, deluge
becak	pedicab
belanda	Dutch, European
bengkel	small repair shop, workshop
bersiap, bersiaptijd	Bersiap or bersiaptijd is the Dutch-Indisch name used for the early months of the Indonesian national revolution that followed the end of World War II. Derived from the Indonesian *bersiap,* "get ready" or "be prepared." The bersiap is generally considered to have lasted from August 1945 to early 1946.
bolos	escape, be absent

cabe rawit	small chili peppers
cicak	small house lizard
Cina	Chinese person (somewhat derogatory)
desa	rural village
gedek	panel or wall made of woven bamboo
gudang	storage room, warehouse
gula jawa	local palm sugar
heiho	(Japanese) Indonesian military aides
Indo	Eurasian
Inggris	English, English person
jongos	houseboy
kacang hijau	mung beans
kalong	large fruit bat, also known as flying fox or flying dog
kampung	native urban neighborhood
kangkung	edible water spinach
kasti	a kind of softball
kebun	yard, garden; gardener
kenari	Javanese almond
kenpeitai	(Japanese) military police
kipas	bamboo fan
koki	domestic cook
kopiah	untasseled fez of black velvet
kwee	(here) mispronunciation of *kue* (cake, sweet) and *gue* (you)

laron	flying white ant
lebaran	celebration at the end of Ramadan
lekas	quick, fast
lemper	sticky rice cooked in coconut milk with bits of spiced meat, rolled and steamed in a banana leaf
mandi	bathe; bathing vessel or place
mandur	supervisor, foreman
nasi goreng	fried rice
nyonya	married woman, lady, ma'am
obat nyamuk	mosquito repellent or coil
oliebollen	(Dutch) traditional beignets served in the Netherlands around the last week of the year, especially on New Year's Eve
pasar	market, marketplace
pemuda	young male activist, at this time commonly a freedom fighter
perkutut	turtledove
pisang susu	small sweet variety of banana
priyayi	elite, aristocrat
rampokker	(Dutch/Indisch) robber, brigand,
rijsttafel	(Dutch) literally, a "rice table," a dinner that consists of roughly 15–20 small dishes—some spicy, some sweet and sour—served in small amounts around a mound of rice.
romusha	(Japanese) literally, a manual laborer; during the occupation, a forced laborer

ronggeng	(Javanese) female dancer who performs for money at parties
sapu lidi	a broom made of flexible palm-leaf ribs
selamatan	a ceremonial meal or banquet
senang	content, at peace
sinyo	(Portuguese) Caucasian or Eurasian young man
sirih	betel leaves
sopir	chauffeur, driver
spandri	(Dutch/Indisch) soldier close to retirement age who would be put into service for small chores
tangsi	military barracks
tani	farmer, cultivator
tauke	gecko
tempat perlindungan	protected place, shelter
tempo dulu	the "good old [colonial] days"
tikar	sleeping mat
totok	(Javanese) full-blooded
trasi	fermented shrimp paste
Tuan, tuan	Sir, Mr.; a term of respect for older male
ubi	yam
wajan	large, wok-like iron pan
warung	roadside vending or food stall

About the Author

Fred Lanzing was born in 1933 in the city of Bandung, Java, then part of the Netherlands East Indies and now the Republic of Indonesia. His father, Lt. Kol. Louis F. Lanzing (1896–1956), was an Indies-born career officer in the KNIL (Royal Netherlands Indies Army) whose own father and two uncles (Fred's grandfather and great-uncles) had served in the KNIL before him. In the late 1930s, L. F. Lanzing was a high-ranking supply officer, and in 1939 was appointed aide-de-camp to Governor-General A. W. L. Tjarda van Starkenborgh Stachouwer. Young Fred and his family—older sister Carolien (1931–1956) and mother Carolien Lanzing-Fokker (1908–1996)—followed Lt. Kol. Lanzing to his several different postings on Java, and when war became imminent they moved to Batavia (now Jakarta). Although this was in some senses a "military family," they did not live in a military atmosphere at home, and their daily lives were very similar to those of European civilians of the business and professional classes in Java's urban centers. Career officers they may have been, but Fred's father and grandfather were certainly not old colonial warhorses.

When the Dutch colonial government surrendered to Japanese forces in March 1942, Fred Lanzing's father became a military prisoner of war (POW) in the "10th Battalion" (also called "Cycle" or "Bicycle") camp, near Batavia, where he spent the entire war period; he functioned as camp leader and ran a tight ship there. As Fred has recounted in some detail in his memoir of the period, the rest of the family was interned at a series of civilian camps beginning in October 1942. All four were fortunate enough to survive the war without severe harm, and in early 1946 resettled in the Netherlands, where Fred's father retired from the KNIL and took up administrative work.

The family moved to Amsterdam, and young Fred resumed his education. In 1953 he took his national school-leaving exams and hoped to study sociology, but was forced to compromise with his father's disapproval and settled on history. His heart wasn't in it, however, and after a few years he quit his studies and fulfilled his military service, attaining the rank of second lieutenant. Then free to follow his own inclinations, he returned to school, entering the Faculty of Social Sciences at the Gemeente Universiteit (later the national University of Amsterdam), and in 1960 graduated *cum laude* in Sociology and Anthropology. He found work first as a researcher in the personnel management department of a large firm, and then in 1970 as a teacher in a vocational school for social work. Subsequently, he became deputy personnel director and later, after a government-mandated merger of forty such schools, personnel director for the resulting Hogeschool van Amsterdam, an institution of forty thousand students.

In 1992 Fred Lanzing took early retirement, which he has used to continue pursuing his interest in colonial history and writing commentary, historical works, and some fiction on various subjects, particularly concerning Indonesia during the Pacific War. He lives in Amsterdam.

Selected Works by Fred Lanzing

1980 "Geen school, geen schoenen, geen ouders: Autobiografische aantekeningen over soldaten en vaders in Nederlands-Indië" [No school, no shoes, no parents: Autobiographical notes on soldiers and fathers in the Netherlands Indies]. *Maatstaf* 28, 11 (November), 56–77.

1982 "Brief aan Jeroentje van nr. 7" [Letter to Jerry at no. 7]. *NRC Handelsblad,* January 8.

1985 "Heulen met de Vijand: Brief aan een onbekende pemuda" [In league with the enemy: Letter to an unknown Indonesian freedom fighter]. *NRC Handelsblad,* August 16.

1997 *Vannacht gaan wij op pad: Oost-Indische verhalen uit een grimmig verleden* [Tonight we'll get started: East Indies tales from a gruesome past]. Amsterdam: Arbeiderspers.

1997 "De Vragenlijst" [The questionnaire]. In *Vannacht gaan wij op pad,* 168–88.

2002 *Gerucht op de wind* [Rumor]. Schoorl: Conserve.

2005 *Soldaten van smaragd: De wereld van de KNIL* [Emerald soldiers: The world of the KNIL]. Amsterdam: Agustus.

2007 *"Voor Fredje is het kamp een paradijs": Een jeugd in Nederlands-Indië 1933–1946* ["For Freddy camp life is heaven": A childhood in the Dutch East Indies, 1933–1946]. Amsterdam: Augustus.

2009 *De Nisero-affaire* [The affair on the *Nisero*]. Amsterdam: Atlas-Contact.

2010 "Niet meer bedelen om excuses" [No more begging for apologies]. *De Groene Amsterdammer,* August 12.

2013 "Heksen, geesten, spoken, weerwolven en broeders" [Witches, ghosts, phantoms, werewolves, and priests]. In *Ellendige leven:*

　　　　　Nederlandse schrijvers in de negentiende eeuw [Miserable lives: Dutch writers on the nineteenth century], edited by Rick Honings and Olf Praamstra, 267–76. Hilversum: Verlorens.

2014　　*Toean Nippon: De Japanse soldaat in de pacific-oorlog en in Nederlands-Indië, 1942–1947* [Mr. Japan: The Japanese soldier in the Pacific War and in the Netherlands Indies, 1942–1947]. Hilversum: Rombus.

Index

Adek (Algemeen Delisch Emigratie Kantoor, General Deli Emigration Office) (camp), 67–68
Al, Joop B. (1930–), 99
Alcantara (ship), 75–79, 80
Ataka (Egyptian port), 81

Baden-Powell, Robert (1857–1941), 105
Bandung, 61–63, 102
Bathing Beauty (film, 1944, George Sidney), 77
Batavia, 13–28, 62, 101; Japanese occupy, 25, 35. *See also* Jakarta
Beatrix, Queen of the Netherlands (1938– , r. 1980–2003), 95
Beetje Oorlog, Een (A little bit of war) (Nieuwenhuis), 95
Bezonken Rood (Brouwers), xviii, 37, 95–96, 103
Black Cat, The (nightclub), 21
Boomslot (Cimahi camp leader), 48–60 passim
Brouwers, Jeroen (Jeroentje) (1940–), xviii, 37–38, 95–96, 103
Buitenzorg (Bogor), 8–12
Burroughs, Edgar Rice (1875–1950), 17

Chinese, 5, 6, 16, 20, 21, 32, 33, 70
Cideng (camp), 34, 35–42 passim, 83–84, 95–96, 103–5; according to Brouwers, 37–38, 43; condition at war's end, 64; not a typical internment camp, xviii
Cikini (swimming pool), 23
Cimahi (camp), 46–47, 48–60 passim, 105–6, 108
colonial life and society in prewar Java, 1–3 and passim; European clubs and entertainment, 18–20; in a European household, 14–16; markets, 21; pigeon racing, 22–23; servants, 14, 16–17; on tea plantation, 9–10
Courier of the Czar (i.e., *Mikhail Strogoff, Courier of the Czar*) (Verne), 54

decolonization issues in the Netherlands, xv, 98
Deventer, Conrad Theodor van (1857–1915), 90

East Indies Camp Syndrome (*OostIndisch Kampsyndroom*), xvi
émigrés from the Netherlands East Indies, postwar: Dutch treatment of, xiv, 81–83, 88, 100; traumas and issues in the Netherlands, xiv, 81, 90–91; waves of, xiv, 93–95
Eurasians, xiv, 21, 32, 40, 49, 51, 70, 76–77, 88–89, 94, 112, 113

Flash Gordon (comic), 17
food: on repatriation ship, 74, 78; supply at end of war, 59, 62, 65, 107, 109, 111; supply in camps, xvi, xviii, xx, 35, 37, 40, 49–51, 55, 59, 71, 84, 110, 112

Gemeente Universiteit (Municipal University) 87, 122
Germans, in prewar Java, 20
Glodok prison, 85

Hillen, Ernest (1936–), xx, 95
Hirohito (Emperor Shōwa) (1901–1989), 95

Hiroshima, 57–58
Hogeschool van Amsterdam, 122
Hong Kong, xxi
Hop (Cimahi camp assistant leader), 48–60 passim

immigration. *See* émigrés from the Netherlands East Indies, postwar
indemnity issue, 111–13
Indians (British Indian civilians), "Bombayans," 21, 32–33
Indies Question (Indische Kwestie), xv
Indos. *See* Eurasians
internees, civilian: attitudes toward Japanese, xxi; clash of cultures, 27; in Java, 29–67 passim; memoirs and autobiographical accounts, xix, 94, 99; in Netherlands East Indies, xiv; in Southeast Asia, xiii–xiv; postwar circumstances in Java, xiv–xxii, 59, 64, 78, 106–7; as victims, 88, 97–115 passim
internees, military: Dutch, 44, 45, 66, 121; European in Southeast Asia, xiii; Italian (in Egypt), 81; Japanese, 74
internment camps, Java: Adek, 67–68; children's life in, 35–36, 55; Cideng, 34, 35–42, 37–38, 43, 108; Cimahi, 46–47, 48–60, 104, 105–6; compared with German concentration camps, xix, 84, 95; disputes about, xxii; food situation, 37, 49–51, 59, 110, 111–12; health issues, 39, 51–53, 112–13; Kramat, 29–34, 35; money in 35, 103; myths about, xxii, 95–96, 103; nature of, xviii; placed under military control, 36; postwar situation in, 59, 106–7; as protected areas, 29, 102; roll calls, 53, 107–8; servants allowed in, 30, 35, 103; sexual issues, 45, 105; Tangerang, 43–47, 104, 108; Tenth Battalion, 69–71, 83
internment of Europeans on Java: begins, 29, 102; ethnic differences as factor, 29; purpose of, 30
Islam: and cats, 18; and pork, 5

Jakarta, 63, 64–66, 121; postwar disorder in, 63, 65, 69–71, 70. *See also* Batavia
Jan, Uncle (cousin of L. F. Lanzing), 32, 34
Jan Lighthart School, 13
Japanese: civilians prewar, 20; Dutch attitudes toward before internment, 26, 29; myths about, 23, soldiers, 25–27, 51, 103, 106; soldiers and children, 27
Japanese Americans, 114
Japanese occupation of Java: clichés, xix; disputed issues, xv, 87–91; long-term effects of, xxii; study of, xiii, xxii, 87–90, 98–100
JES. *See* Stichting Japanse Ereschulden (Foundation for Japanese Debts of Honor)

KNIL (Koninklijk Nederlands Indisch Leger, Royal Netherlands Indies Army), 5, 20, 25, 48, 101–2, 111, 121–22
Kondo (camp commander Cideng to 1 April 1944), 37
Kousbroek, Rudy (1929–2010), xvi
Kramat (camp), 29–34, 35, 102
Kunimoto (Cimahi camp commander), 50–51, 53–54, 107–8, 111–12
KZ genre (Konzentrationslager genre, concentration camp genre), 94–96, 97

Lanzing, Carolien (sister of Fred, 1931–1956), 3, 10, 11, 33, 38, 42, 64, 70, 77–78, 102, 121
Lanzing, Fred (1933–), passim; accuracy of memoir, xvii–xix; in Amsterdam, 87, 122; arrival in Holland, 80–81; biography, 121–22; critics of, xvii, 91, 97; earlier works, xvi–xvii; 33; leaves Java for Holland, 74–79; reflections on Dutch colonialism, 101; visits postwar Japan, 57–58
Lanzing, Louis F. (father of Fred, 1896–1956), 3, 7, 10, 25, 30, 64, 66, 69, 70, 77–79, 102, 121

Lanzing-Fokker, Carolien (mother of Fred, 1908–1996), 3, 21, 30, 33, 38, 42, 46, 64, 70, 77, 102, 121
Lechner, Jan (1927–), xx

Manila, xxi
May, Karl (1842–1912), 54
memory wars, xv, xxii
Mountbatten, Edwina (wife of Louis) (1901–1960), 64
Mountbatten, Louis (1900–1979), 59

Nagasaki, 57–58
nationalism, Indonesian, 59
New Amsterdam (ship), 70, 71
Nieuwenhuis, Rob (1908–1999), 95
NIROM (Nederlandsch-Indische Radio-omroepmaatschappij, Dutch East Indies Radio Broadcasting Corporation), 11
NSB (Nationaal Socialistische Beweging, National Socialist Movement), 82

Oostindische Kampsyndroom (term and book) (Kousbroek), xvi

Post, Laurens van der Post (1906–1996), xix, 69
POWs. *See* internees, military
Prince of Wales (ship), 12

radios: sealed by Japanese, 29, 31; secret, in camp Cimahi, 57
RAPWI (Recovery of Allied Prisoners of War and Internees), 78
Red Cross, 66
Repulse (ship), 12
Rijksmuseum (1976 exhibition), 87
Rijnlands Lyceum (Wassenaar), 82

sailors: British, 75, 77–78; British Indian, 72
San Francisco Peace Treaty, 96
Singapore, 12, 72, 74
Snouck Hurgronje, Christiaan (1857–1936), 18
soldiers: British, 74; British Indian, 71; British Indian Gurkhas, 61–63, 111; British Indian Sikhs, 67–68; Indonesian freedom fighters (extremists, militia, *pemuda*), 30, 61, 62, 65, 68, 71, 88, 109; Indonesian *heiho*, 45, 46–47, 52, 108, 110–11; Japanese, 25–27, 47, 51, 103, 106; KNIL, Europeans, 69; KNIL, Moluccans, 69–70, 99; Korean, 51–53, 55–57, 59, 107
Sone Kenichi (1910?–1946), xvi, 30, 38–42, 47, 56; appearance, 38; biography of, 83–86; Fred Lanzing treated by, 39–41; harshness of, 40–41; house of, 39, 41; mistress of, 40; policies of, 40; rages of, 40, 84; court-martial and execution, 84–86
Stichting Japanse Ereschulden (Foundation for Japanese Debts of Honor, JES), 90, 96, questionnaire, 97–115; criticism of, 113
Stichting Jongens in de Japanse Kampen '42–'45 (Foundation for Boys from the Japanese Camps, '42–'45), 90
Stichting Pelita (Pelita Foundation), 91
Suharto (1921–2008), 8
Sukarno (1901–1970), 8, 17
Surabaya, 4–9

Tangerang (camp), 43–47; authoritarian regime of, 43–44, 104–5, 108
Tanjung Priok, 70–71
Tarzan of the Apes (Burroughs), 17
Tenth (10th) Battalion (camp), 69–71, 83, 121
Tjarda van Starkenborgh Stachouwer, A.W.L. (1888–1978), 3, 6, 7, 9, 64, 121
Twenty Thousand Leagues under the Sea (Verne), 38

Uit de Verte: Een jeugd in Indië (Lechner), xx

Velden, Doetje (Dora) van (1909–1997), xviii
Vereniging van Kinderen uit de Japanse Bezetting en Bersiap (Childen of the Japanese Occupation and the Bersiap), 90–91
Verne, Jules (1828–1905), 38

war criminals, Japanese, xix
Way of a Boy: A Memoir of Java, The (Hillen), xx, 95
Witt, J(oh)an de (1625–1672), 44
Woman in the Window (film, 1944, Fritz Lang), 77
World War II: comes to Java, 12, 17, 23, 24; ends in Japan, 57–58; ends in Java, 59, 106; German occupation of the Netherlands, xiv, 8, 93; memories of in the Netherlands, xiii–xiv; news of European war in Java, 29; preparations for in Netherlands East Indies, 23

Yoshida-Stikker Protocol, 90, 96
Yoshizawa Kenkichi (1874–1965), 6

www.ingramcontent.com/pod-product-compliance
Lightning Source LLC
Chambersburg PA
CBHW020654300426
44112CB00007B/379